FIND YOUR SWEET SPOT

A Guide to Personal and Professional Excellence

Karen Elizaga

Guilford, Connecticut
An imprint of Globe Pequot Press

To buy books in quantity for corporate use
or incentives, call **(800) 962-0973**
or e-mail **premiums@GlobePequot.com**.

 skirt!® is an attitude . . . spirited, independent, outspoken, serious, playful and irreverent, sometimes controversial, always passionate.

skirt!® is an imprint of Globe Pequot Press.
skirt! ® is a registered trademark of Morris Book Publishing, LLC, and is used with express permission.

Text design: Sheryl Kober
Layout: Kirsten Livingston
Project editor: Ellen Urban

Library of Congress Cataloging-in-Publication Data

Elizaga, Karen.
 Find your sweet spot : a guide to personal and professional excellence
/ Karen Elizaga.
    pages cm
 Includes bibliographical references and index.
 ISBN 978-0-7627-9187-3 (hardback)
 1. Women—Vocational guidance. 2. Career development. 3. Success.
I. Title.
 HF5382.6.E45 2014
 650.1—dc23

                                                    2013026847

Printed in the United States of America

10 9 8 7 6 5 4 3 2 1

For Sloane and Finn

Every day, you inspire me to aspire to excellence.

"The soul walks not upon a line,
neither does it grow like a reed.
The soul unfolds itself,
like a lotus of countless petals."

—Kahlil Gibran, *The Prophet*

Contents

Foreword

Bill Cowher and Queen V here. When our friend Karen Elizaga first described what would ultimately become *Find Your Sweet Spot,* her ideas and techniques piqued our interest. We couldn't wait to read about them. Now that we have, we are excited to share the good news. Here is a book that can help you achieve your goals, no matter what your passion or profession. Even though we've spent our careers in entirely different industries—as a former head coach of the Pittsburgh Steelers and as an independent rock artist and entrepreneur, respectively—Karen's insights and coaching techniques resonated deeply with both of us.

I, Bill, have given hundreds of speeches on leadership to companies, teams, and organizations based on my personal life and professional experiences. And I, Veronica, have always striven to send out a message of self-empowerment, whether on or off stage, leading a band, or running my record label.

Despite our disparate backgrounds, we each found *Find Your Sweet Spot* to be an excellent resource for ourselves and for anyone in search of mindful living, regardless of gender, age, or station in life. In a time where self-help books line the shelves, this book stands out not only because of Karen's unique background and worldview, but also because her recommendations draw from her professional coaching practice with her vast and diverse clientele.

Like Karen, we've worked with men and women of diverse backgrounds and skills and found that *Find Your Sweet Spot* has real applicability across the board. *Find Your Sweet Spot* offers a positive approach to dealing with the challenges of daily life, as well as specific techniques for making the necessary changes that can lead to excellent living. Karen addresses mental and emotional states as well as physical well-being, and then ties it all together. We have found Karen's holistic view to be universally relevant yet, inexplicably, often overlooked. Her "sweet spot" strategies work!

Not only that, but they are easy to incorporate. Throughout her book, Karen introduces a variety of thought-provoking exercises that are simple and quick enough to practice every day. After reading *Find Your Sweet Spot,* a number of the recommended actions, such as Detox Your Vocab and Practice Gratitude, still remain with us; we find them popping up at unexpected times, lifting our quality of life on a daily basis.

We both found the book to be such an enjoyable read. As we turned the pages, it felt like we were sitting with Karen in person. She and her book have made a positive impact on our lives, helping us to appreciate what we have and inspiring us to strive to be better people. Read on and see what she and this book can do for you!

—Bill Cowher, former NFL head coach
of the Pittsburgh Steelers and CBS analyst

—Veronica Stigeler, songwriter and recording artist
professionally known as Queen V

Introduction

Imagine waking up refreshed from a good night's sleep. You open your eyes to a day that feels bright with possibility, filled with the activities and the people you love. Imagine teeming with gratitude and pride for the life you've created and bounding out of bed to greet it. When was the last time you experienced this? As a child? In your dreams? Can't remember?

Instead, tell me if this sounds familiar. Your alarm goes off, and with your eyes squeezed tight to shut out the creeping daylight, you grope for the snooze button.

Just a few more minutes, please!

You wish you could stay in bed for just a little—or a lot—longer. You have a sinking feeling that the day ahead is packed with tedious tasks. Even as you try to catch some extra slumber, your mind begins to race through your to-do list, which only confirms your lack of inspiration.

Sigh.

You reach down and rest your hands on your belly: it's bloated. You feel some guilt and annoyance with yourself about what you ate and drank last night. Exhaling another burdened sigh, you finally rise from bed, your body aching with fatigue.

No matter . . . you must begin your day. In a rush, you skip breakfast, forgo any form of a workout or meditation, and hurry off to drop the kids at school or to get right to the office. Traffic annoys you. And then someone puts an unpleasant chink in your morning by saying something, intentionally or not, that stings. It sticks with you all day.

I should have just stayed home.

Now, everything really irritates you. The day just plain stinks. As you go along, you make unhealthy food choices, reaching for the quickest fix, probably something processed and lacking nutrition. In fact, you feel even more sluggish after you eat, not to mention the sense of failure you harbor because you've wrecked your healthy plan. Now, you might even need that cigarette.

I'll quit tomorrow.

You find your job unfulfilling; you're disengaged. You're so tired or bored, or both, that you keep running to the coffee shop for those caffeine boosts that help you get through the long hours. Or, perhaps, you are so driven to achieve that you forget to eat or take any breaks. As the day continues, you wonder why you can't seem to get it right. Your to-do list grows by the hour, and while you may enjoy fleeting moments of happiness, the day leaves you feeling depleted. Frazzled.

To cap it all off, you wash down a large, greasy dinner with a giant, sugary cocktail. You certainly need it. Surely, you deserve it.

Sound familiar? Do little things irk you and then add up so that it all gets to you in a big way? Does one rough moment lead to another, until you can't get out from under it? As you ruminate about your subpar life, do you tend to assume that others have it so much better?

Not anymore. This book will help you to walk away from days like these. As I have helped so many of my clients, I will help you to discover your sweet spot—that wellspring of energy, joy, and fulfillment.

But wait! Maybe you're thinking, *Hey, my life is okay. It's actually pretty good—at least better than what you just described. That's awful!* What now? This book is *still* for you. Finding your sweet spot will kick your game up several notches, bringing excellence to everything you do.

Have you ever taken the time to determine what comprises your sweet spot? Have you thought about how healthy habits and strategies can support and feed the energy necessary to lead a satisfying life? If not, it's highly probable that you go through your days doing what you feel you *ought* to do, rather than what you *want* to do. It's also likely that, even if you *are* doing more or less what you want to be doing, you lack the energy to sustain growth and excellence in your chosen field, or in your personal life.

Years ago, my husband, Jay, had a lightbulb moment. He realized that when people passed him in his office hallways and greeted him with the perfunctory, "Hey, how are you?" he felt more than the perfunctory, "Fine, thanks" or "Okay." In fact, when he actually paused to consider the question that day, he realized his feelings well exceeded the standard reply. He started to respond, "Great!" and "Fantastic!"—often to the surprise of his colleagues.

Sure, "Okay" and "Fine" are certainly better than some alternatives, but these widely accepted defaults don't need to set the bar for how we live. Beyond okay, there *is* "Great!" Beyond okay, there's real joy, vitality, and a career or lifestyle that you love and that really fits the unique person you are. Beyond fine, you can find balance and feel fantastic—elated, even—in your physical body, in your emotional state, and in your soul. Even during very challenging times, you can draw real strength and comfort from your sweet spot.

The thing is, unless we give ourselves time and space to think about how we *want* to live, we end up just muddling or racing through our days unaware of our potential for excellence. If we don't give ourselves a chance to have our own lightbulb moments, we either accept the status quo or, worse, complain incessantly about it. Sometimes, we arrive at our epiphanies only after years of struggling through it. When my clients stop to think honestly about how they live versus how they *want* to live, they experience their own aha moments and then begin to take action to move beyond just okay.

Give yourself a moment. Find your sweet spot, exit this mode of just okay, and open the floodgates to excellence. Make the way you want to live your life, which may at times seem lofty and elusive, accessible. By following the Sweet Spot Checks in this book with some consistent effort, you *will* find your own sweet spot.

* * * * *

I didn't happen upon these sweet spot strategies by accident. This book is the result of my research, coaching studies at New York University, as well as experience working with more than a thousand people from different walks of life. As an executive coach, I use a holistic approach in my work with top-level executives in large companies in cities such as Los Angeles, New York, and London. They hire me to help them evolve and inspire others to produce their best work. Some of these executives have come to me with what others thought were unsolvable issues, teetering on the brink of being let go; some have simply wanted to fine-tune their performance.

Whatever the case, by implementing the very same strategies that I outline in this book, all of my clients have ended up turning things around, changing others' perceptions of them, and making massive strides forward and upward. They have also learned tactics for embracing and exuding confidence, communicating more effectively, and looking and feeling great. Most importantly, despite initial doubt that change was even possible, these clients have discovered their own sweet spots, experiencing personal fulfillment and improved relationships in the process.

I also help non-executive clients to determine optimal paths forward. Among them are young adults navigating their way out of college and graduate school, mothers looking to dive (or at least dip their toes) back into the workforce, and individuals simply wanting to carve out new directions. Some are looking for love; others want to lose weight; still others yearn for significant career changes. In all cases, we define concrete goals and lay out action plans; then, within months, these individuals are thrilled to experience desired change. They build up their confidence and move past the self-limiting beliefs that previously quashed their potential.

I also teach students, from primary school to high school, to develop skills and a strong sense of their intrinsic value, effectively paving the way for happiness and success. Thus equipped, these young people have gone on to lead fulfilling lives, forging healthy relationships and contributing meaningfully to society. In my workshops, students learn to cultivate love for themselves and leave with a crystal-clear picture of how they want their lives to turn out. While I know that for many of them, goals and interests will shift over time, I'm confident that they now have the tools they will need to follow their inner compass. Over the years, I've received hundreds of e-mails from students expressing genuine appreciation for the work we've done together. I am so grateful for the positive feedback. My clients inspire me to hone my coaching skills and fuel my sweet spot every day!

I've coached people from all kinds of backgrounds—of all shapes, sizes, colors, and persuasions—and the strategies, which you'll find here, have worked across the board. By implementing these strategies, my clients have lifted themselves up and out of extremely challenging situations and forged their own paths to genuine contentment. When you boil it down, my job is to be evocative and provocative—to evoke the excellent ideas teeming within people and to provoke insights and epiphanies. To make the ideas stick, I ask my clients probing questions to come up with action items and furnish them with strategies just like the Sweet Spot Checks in this book, to solidify lessons and aha moments. With this book, you now have access to the same privileged information that my personal clients do.

• • • • •

I feel fortunate. Somehow, I found the courage to live and breathe in my own sweet spot. But it took me years to discover it, and yet a few more to find the nerve to honor it. Although my days aren't always easy, they certainly flow a lot more smoothly than they used to.

In retrospect, I can admit that I spent many years—decades, even—toeing the gap between how I lived and what I actually wanted. I devoured self-help and psychology books, attended self-improvement seminars, experimented with hypnosis and the latest diet crazes, and brainstormed (or sometimes flat-out commiserated) with friends and colleagues about how to achieve something, *anything*, better. Although I worked hard to maintain appearances to the contrary, my journey to my own sweet spot was far from a cakewalk. I found it challenging to "walk the talk," and I sometimes veered off the path and struggled to find it again.

I grew up in laid-back Honolulu, but as the firstborn child of two well-educated immigrants (including one doctor) who left their families in the Philippines for a better life in the United States, I felt a lot of pressure to be successful, to strive for perfection. No questions asked. So I spent much of my childhood envisioning a professional life, specifically as a doctor. Unfortunately, I sucked at math, I despised science, and, in my heart of hearts, I had no desire to pursue medicine.

Beyond the expectations of my own family, there was this larger societal pressure. I understood this immutable fact: Filipino kids of Filipino immigrant doctors become doctors themselves. I can't tell you the number of times that my father's friends (yes, all Filipino, and all doctors) asked me whether I would take over his internal medicine and hematology practice.

Blood? Blech!

What was my alternative? I know, I could become a lawyer!

Graduate school. Check.

Doctorate. Check.

No chemistry. Good.

No math. Excellent.

And I would be a financial success. *Ka-ching!*

Most importantly, I'd make my parents proud.

The crime of it is that this was my entire analysis. At the tender age of thirteen, I set my sights on a law school for no other reason than I could be a "doctor" without being "Doc." I didn't know what I was good at, or even what my weaknesses were. The concept of a sweet spot eluded me completely. In fact, it took another thirteen years for me to realize—when I was knee-deep in legal documents at a New York law firm and feeding my hungry soul a steady stream of chocolate to compensate—that in fact my sweet spot, whatever it was, did *not* live within the four walls of a law firm. My epiphany went like this:

I like:
- being with people
- talking to people

- finding out what motivates people
- meeting new people
- connecting people
- encouraging people to achieve their dreams
- inspiring people to think differently and productively
- helping people to achieve their goals
- constantly learning how people think and evolve

I *don't* like:
- being by myself
- boredom
- conflict
- negotiating in tough, adversarial situations
- in fact, negotiating at all
- routine
- lack of creativity

What I did as a lawyer:
- sat in my office by myself
- revised formulaic documents
- negotiated contentious provisions
- researched
- wrote legal memos

Here, I was miles away from my sweet spot. Sure, I was good at my job, but I certainly didn't love it. And I had no clue about how to appreciate my life. The result? I was unhappy and disengaged at work. As I consistently worked unreasonably long hours, disenchantment corroded my personal life. Without exception, I sabotaged my daily diligent efforts at the gym by filling my body with unhealthy foods and a perennial stash of chocolate in my desk drawer. The cycle continued: I spent scads of time and psychic energy contemplating what I would eat and how it would make me feel; then I would eat junk, beat myself up afterward, and despise my reflection in the mirror.

Can you imagine how much time, energy, and brain space that ate up? Way too much.

Nor did I know much about nutrition and how my standard American diet fueled the vicious cycle. I didn't evaluate the other unproductive habits, such as fixating on the negative and judging myself harshly, that were staples in my life. I was quite literally giving my life over to a mediocre existence.

To others, given my career and polished outward appearance, I seemed to have my act together. In fact, I did have reasons to be happy. For example, I enjoyed a beautiful relationship with my husband, who has been my partner ever since. But it was my tendency to focus on what was wrong with my life that made me unhappy under the shiny surface. Negativity dominated my conscious thoughts, undermining whatever goodness was in my life. Can you relate?

Then in 2003, while living in London, I gave birth to my daughter, Sloane. For me, she was a powerful catalyst for real and genuine growth. Now, with an innocent baby girl, I couldn't go on being stuck in this vicious cycle. No way! As Sloane's mother, I realized I needed to do something. The birth of Finn three and a half years later, back in New York City, when I was well into my journey toward my sweet spot, was the nail in the coffin of "just okay." Responsible for two young lives, I *really* needed and wanted to be my best self. I craved excellence in all aspects of my life.

Yes, I've found my sweet spot. That stash of chocolate? I can't believe I needed it. The cycle is gone. The difference between my habitual thoughts and feelings back then and what they are now is stunning. Ever since I off-loaded tremendous negative energy, and learned to manage it on a daily basis, life is definitely sweeter!

I want you to experience the very same thing. In this book, I will help you to discover (or rediscover, as the case may be) your sweet spot. Because I know for a fact that each and every one of us has one. No matter how you deal with challenges or navigate your life now, you are capable of extraordinary change and personal evolution.

Will you benefit from this book if you just blaze through it, without pausing to do the exercises? Surely! People have told me that simply reading this book helped them to feel better and aspire to more. But the way to get the *most* out of this book is to read a few chapters at a time, completing the Sweet Spot Checks, reading on, and then doing more Sweet Spot Checks—until you've completed them all. Then, using the book as a reference, you can always page back to the sections that are most relevant to you at any given moment. That's how I wrote it, and it's actually how I live my life. From day to day, challenges inevitably arise, but our Sweet Spot Checks are always at the ready.

Make an effort to read the whole book from beginning to end, for it follows a logical sequence that I've found most effective in my practice. Don't let yourself miss out on all the tips, tricks, and inspirational stories throughout. Whether you maintain the status quo, make just a few small but vital tweaks, or undergo a major overhaul in your life, it's entirely up to you. Give yourself the luxury of choice by absorbing the information in the following pages and then deciding how you will use it.

As you read on, consider what your catalysts for change are. For me, it was becoming a mother to my two beautiful children, and for that I am forever grateful to them. For you, it might be something else, and it might not be quite as obvious. But *something* has motivated you to pick up this book. What is it?

When you find your sweet spot, you will experience what my clients and I have—a delicious unfolding of self-acceptance, confidence, joy, fulfillment, and excellence. No matter how okay, miserable, or just plain stuck you might feel right now, you are capable of dramatic change. So clear the decks and take this journey. See what's in store for you and how much brighter your days can be!

Part I

The Sweet
Spot Strategy

"Tell your heart that the fear of suffering is
worse than the suffering itself. And that
no heart has ever suffered when it goes
in search of its dreams . . ."

—Paulo Coelho, *The Alchemist*

Discover Your Sweet Spot

In tennis, it's certainly possible to whack the ball over the net any old way. But have you ever hit the ball (or witnessed someone hit it) right in the special zone that makes that satisfying *POP!* sound? When you find that spot, the ball sails fast and clean exactly where you want it. As you get into the rhythm of your sweet spot—your mind calm and clear, your body a finely tuned instrument of agility and muscle memory—you really start to enjoy yourself. It becomes fulfilling, and you want to play for as long as possible, no matter how sweaty, thirsty, or winded you might get. Your actions flow. Even if you don't win the match, you feel fantastic while you're at it. Hello, sweet spot!

Mihaly Csikszentmihalyi, a world-renowned psychologist and researcher on positive psychology, calls this concept "flow," where "people become so involved in what they are doing that the activity becomes spontaneous, almost automatic; they stop being aware of themselves as separate from the actions they are performing" (*Flow*, p. 53). There's power in that flow. *That's* the power of the sweet spot. Energy, ease, and excellence. A healthy desire to keep going, no matter what, because it's so satisfying.

Csikszentmihalyi talks about flow in the context of an activity, but I am talking about applying the phenomenon to life itself. How? Go within. When you do, you recognize your sweet spot as that unique place where you feel the most vital and alive. Here, your body feels strong, full of health and energy. Your heart teems with love, radiating from a well-cultivated core of self-love and extending out to others. Your brain and heart, skilled with sweet spot strategies, infuse your whole being with positive messages that keep you motivated, focused, and joyful on this singular journey that is your life.

When you draw on your sweet spot, you find the confidence to navigate any situation and the tenacity to pursue your goals, despite adversity. You recognize your potential, which allows you to self-actualize with clarity and optimism. You become adept at managing your time, maximizing growth and productivity in the areas that matter most to you while maintaining inner balance. You engage others and have the wherewithal to seize intriguing opportunities. Moment by moment, day by day, you are able to savor all the goodness and beauty in your life. You live authentically according to the person that you are. Quite simply, you function at your personal best. *That's* your sweet spot. Yes, your own. When you find it, stay true to it!

I know many lucky people who work *and* live in their sweet spots. It took me years, a series of trials, errors, and difficult lessons, to find and then embrace my sweet spot. Now, as a result, I get to do those things that come naturally to me, that I love, so that my day-to-day life—even work—feels like play. I feel energized, not drained, and I am optimistic about what life will bring. And even in those difficult, seemingly insurmountable moments (yes, I have those, too), I rely on my sweet spot strategies to find balance and create solutions. I want this for you.

Journey to Your Sweet Spot

Now it's your turn to tell your story and create a new way forward. Throughout the book, I provide what I call Sweet Spot Checks and Sweet Spot Tips, devised to encourage you first to look inward, define your sweet spot, and achieve excellence. Once you have discovered your sweet spot, you can always revisit these exercises and implement the various tips and tools when you need them.

Whether your sweet spot has been hiding from you or you have been hiding from it, you are most likely within reach of it. Your journey begins inside, with establishing a strong foundation of love, confidence, and gratitude. This foundation is essential to your progress. Imagine building the foundation of your dream home. In its construction, wouldn't you be sure to use only the best and sturdiest materials? Therefore, in Part II: Sweet Spot Inside, I've designed the Sweet Spot Checks to help you give your own personal foundation that same attention and effort. Developing a solid foundation to support *you* in all of your endeavors is the first step of the Sweet Spot Strategy.

Once we figure out what's going on inside of you and build on your strengths, we'll work outward, optimizing what you project to the world. Supported by your enhanced foundation, you'll feel and project renewed energy and passion. In Part III: Sweet Spot Outside, you'll gain greater clarity of purpose and discover how you can love what you do and appreciate what you have.

Lastly, in Part IV: Integrate Your Sweet Spot, I'll provide practical strategies for integrating all that you've learned about yourself and your sweet spot to achieve exactly what you want. In addition to building inner fortitude in Part II and strengthening your outward presence in Part III, you will put together all that you've learned into effective follow-through strategies in Part IV—so that you continue to live in your sweet spot, in the face of any challenge.

Throughout the book, as I do with my personal clients, I'll ask you questions to encourage you to examine the person you are: your natural proclivities, your desires, your innate talents. I'll ask you to identify weaknesses, self-doubts, and limiting beliefs and habits that hold you back. I'll ask you to pinpoint reasons to feel great about yourself and your current life. As you complete the Sweet Spot Checks, you'll pave a clear path to your own sweet spot, and your life experience will improve dramatically.

I have worked with people who were complete strangers to their sweet spot, oblivious to their intrinsic value and potential for excellence. In private sessions and in workshop settings, I have encountered all types of professionals—from those who've been labeled as "unsuccessful" or as "failures" to some influential game changers who want to raise their performance up a few notches. Whether you are a full-time parent, a job seeker who's been down on your luck, a posh businessperson with hundreds of demands on your time, or someone simply struggling to find your sweet spot, I assure you, my sweet spot strategy can work for you. You *do* have a sweet spot. You *can* rescue yourself from a life of just muddling through and become a dynamo in your own right. You'll be able to feed your soul—and not with chocolate!

Still, like all good things, finding your sweet spot *is* work. At points, it may even be hard work. It requires honest self-reflection and a real desire to make the necessary changes in your life. Don't be fooled. All those happy people, those beautiful souls, those glittering successes who make it all look so effortless . . . they *are* putting in the work. This is because once you find your sweet spot, you must figure out concrete and creative ways to honor it, align your life with it, and then make adjustments along the way to stay on course. I wrote this book to help you do just that.

I have structured this book in the same way that I structure my work with clients—starting from the inside and working out from there. For the most part, the time-consuming and emotionally intensive exercises come at the beginning, while the much easier exercises and simple tips follow. (That said, the first exercises in each of Parts II, III, and IV are probably the ones you'll get most value from, but they will also require the most effort.)

5

If you are intimidated or overwhelmed by what certain Sweet Spot Checks bring up for you, just take a moment to understand the concepts and then move on. You can come back to them when you feel ready. Keep this book close by so you can access targeted support and guidance as various situations arise.

Change can be scary. Gather the courage, do the work, and embrace the change. Excellence is in the journey, not the destination. It's about growing and learning within your sweet spot, as the unproductive habits, behaviors, and mindsets subside. Living in your sweet spot will buffer the disappointment, stress, or hard luck that comes your way, and it will open doors of opportunity to you that you never thought existed.

Embrace Excellence, Not Perfection

As you undertake the Sweet Spot Checks in this book, know one thing: There is no expectation or requirement that you follow every word to the letter. Certainly, I want you to take real and meaningful action, but you don't need to execute every single directive perfectly.

Sure, the bigger the effort you put forth, the larger the benefit you'll reap, but as we say in my house, "Perfect is for idiots." Why? Perfection is a most elusive standard, meaning different things to different people. Striving for perfection can be counterproductive: No matter how hard we try, we usually fall short. There is no wiggle room in the pursuit of perfection.

Am I suggesting that you settle for average, just satisfactory, or okay? Of course not! In fact, striving for excellence is a much better standard than striving for perfection because incorporated into the former is the space to execute your best effort, make a valiant attempt, and then even *fail* in the process. There is room to experiment, see what happens, and either claim victory or learn valuable lessons from the pursuit. Within excellence, you enjoy flexibility, creativity, and the freedom to question the status quo. The potential for extraordinary results multiplies. Yep, excellence gives you that latitude. Not so with perfection, which breeds a fear of failure—stymieing effort, imagination, and inspiration.

Here's a very simple way to think about perfection and excellence. Imagine a perfect apple. Hold its image in your mind: beautiful, shiny, crisp, unblemished in any way. What happens when you take a bite? Or what if you drop it by accident and it bruises? You've spoiled its perfection. On the other hand, if you imagine that same apple in terms of its inherent excellence, it will remain excellent, whether bitten, bruised, or sauced. There's the flexibility and latitude that doesn't remotely apply to perfection.

Here's another example. Think about marathon runners. Are they stymied by the impossible demands of perfection? No, these runners routinely blow by those impossible demands. Not only do they persevere through the challenging moments (hours!) of the race, but they train and strategize for months leading up to it. They cannot guess the outcome, and chances are very slim that any one of them will come in first place, but they are going to do their darnedest. They strive for personal excellence.

One year, at the 13.5-mile mark of the ING New York City Marathon, I saw an elaborately costumed Captain America run by, as well as a woman holding a tray of cocktails and another man bearing a full-sized American flag on a flagpole. The runners came in all shapes and sizes—tall, thin, heavy, blind (yes, blind!), prosthetic-wearing, young, old, women, men—every type you could imagine.

At 23.5 miles, I saw these same runners. Captain America. Cocktail lady. Blind guy. Prosthetic chick. Flag dude. They had run ten miles from Queens, up and through the Bronx, and back down into Manhattan. Me? I'd walked, taken two subways, and driven a car to get to the same destination. This got me thinking about what it takes to achieve our goals. What *does* it take? Effort. Passion. Good humor. Determined action and a total disregard for attaining perfection.

Do you attempt your goals because you know you will achieve exactly what you want? Or do you shy away from taking that first step because you're afraid you won't be able to achieve your goal exactly as you picture it? Do you start, veer off course, and then give up entirely, or do you persevere? Marathon runners get themselves to the starting line and then they keep going. No excuses. That's excellence right there.

Think about your own pursuit. Do you want to start a business? Do you want to leave your job for something more fulfilling? Do you want to play the piano? Do you want to be fit and healthy? Find a loving relationship? Run a marathon? Whatever your dream is, invest your energies in what's possible rather than defaulting to an all-or-nothing mindset. Many of my clients come to me in fear of suboptimal results, refusing to take action and therefore stuck with the status quo. Friends and clients have complained to me that they don't bother eating well or exercising because they just can't commit to it 100 percent. They can't do it perfectly, they think, so why bother?

Again, to be blunt, perfect is for idiots. Striving for perfection too often means avoiding risk and losing out on great reward. It also stifles creativity, joy, and laughter, which are essential to finding your sweet spot. Excellence is in the journey, and no journey is perfect. What does your excellence look like?

Entertain a Single Thought

Research shows that the human mind is capable of housing only one conscious thought at a time. According to my friend and neuro-psychologist, Dr. Lauren Kwon Dawson, "The brain is an incredible multitasker, simultaneously tending to multiple functions, sensations, and activities each second. However, as it relates to holding a 'conscious thought' per se (excluding all the various philosophical interpretations of what a 'conscious thought' is), we hold a singular cognition at a time."

Try it. Think of one thing—it can be anything: what you're having for dinner tonight, a book you just read, what someone said to you on the phone yesterday. Once you've settled upon that one thought, try to inject another thought into your brain while holding on to the original one. Go ahead. Hold that first thought tightly, and then bring in something new at the very same time. Or, the next time you have a meal with a friend, try to focus on what she is telling you while eavesdropping on the conversation at the next table. Impossible, right? Or try this: Say the alphabet and count to twenty in your head—at exactly the same time, not one right after the other, and not alternating letters with numbers. You'll see that having two simultaneous and very elementary thoughts in your head is quite impossible.

Although your brain cannot consciously house multiple thoughts at the very same time, it certainly can entertain a *series* of thoughts one right after the other. I have designed many of my sweet spot principles off that premise. At any given time, you can make the conscious decision to swap out a negative thought or feeling by inserting into your mind, instead, a single positive and productive reflection.

According to Dr. Dawson, "This practice perfectly embodies the principles in psychology linking our thoughts with our feelings and the importance of having a positive thought to enhance our mood." The nature and quality of your thoughts have a direct correlation to how you feel. Hold onto that thought as you journey to your sweet spot.

Shift Your Perspective

My friends giggle at me when they discover that I regularly walk laps around a parking lot. Yes, multiple laps on hot, cracked, uneven asphalt dotted with goose excrement. I know, it doesn't sound appealing. But it's a beach parking lot that sits fairly empty down the road from my house, and it's surrounded by natural beauty.

Having grown up ten minutes from Waikiki Beach, I am still a local Hawaii girl at heart. I love the water. Looking at it, I find serenity and calm. The way the day's first sun shimmers on the water infuses me with gratitude. During every walk, I can't help but count my blessings.

Until only recently, every time I entered the parking lot, I briskly walked five laps in the same direction before seeking shade. Along this path, I would run into the same gaggle of geese, then take note of the bright ocean kayaks stacked in orange, blue, yellow, and green; next, I'd pass two formidable cannons pointing out toward Long Island, relics of the American Revolutionary War. Meanwhile, I'd also cross paths with other walkers with whom I'd exchange smiles and "good morning" greetings. It's just the way I'd always done it.

It's not unusual for a friend to join me for my morning excursion. One morning, though, panting for air as we gabbed, my friend nudged me in the opposite direction. I felt my body resist at first—this was the wrong way! But I somehow managed to relax into this reverse course and continue on: first, the Minutemen cannons, then the stacks of brightly colored ocean kayaks, and soon the gaggle of geese. Surprised by the simple novelty of this approach, I laughed to myself as my friend's route jolted me into appreciating the beauty of the exact same sights from a different perspective. This way around, I noticed even *more* blue water, more gorgeous houses that pepper the coast, and charming sailboats moored in the marina. More beauty than I'd ever noticed before in that same silly parking lot.

What had changed? Only a simple shift in perspective. A nudge in a new direction. This seemingly insignificant adjustment had a profound impact on my morning routine, enhancing my experience of happiness and gratitude.

In this book, I often invoke the power of perspective. I reflect on the life that so many of us want—one rich with meaning, fulfillment, energy, health, connection, laughter, fun, financial success, discovery, recognition, and joy. The list goes on, but even the goals on this short list may feel unattainable as we go through our daily routines. Most of us are so busy just getting by that we forget that we aspire to be better or simply to be present for the moments of peace, fulfillment, and gratitude that often seem so elusive. But are they so elusive, or are we just approaching our days and our goals from the wrong direction? If we were to try a different route, might we discover that we already have much of what we desire?

What are you paying attention to in your life, and from what perspective? Given the time to think about it, you might realize that you regularly overlook many positive aspects of your life and magnify many of the negative ones. (I used to be an expert at that, remember?) You might have overlooked your sweet spot! Don't miss out on all the goodness that's already within your grasp.

Just as my friend shifted my perspective with a friendly nudge in a different direction, I will help you to discover a new direction and to see your life in extraordinarily fresh colors. So come, walk with me. Your sweet spot awaits!

Part II

The Sweet Spot
Inside

"You yourself, as much as anybody in the entire
universe, deserve your love and affection."

—Buddha

In Part II, The Sweet Spot Inside, I want you to dig deep. Look closely at the person you are. What drives you? What motivates you? How much do you appreciate who you are, flaws and all? Here's your opportunity to strengthen your personal foundation and to determine how you can thrive in your sweet spot.

Cultivate Self-Love

In my practice, I work with top-flight CEOs. You can imagine their reactions when I ask them to what extent they have authentic love for themselves. They look at me as though I have three heads. They want to run away. What's love got to do with executive coaching? Love's got everything to do with everything! Love is the number one ingredient that fuels your sweet spot, enabling you to navigate your life with ease and excellence. And yet, love for ourselves is the number one thing that we overlook.

On Valentine's Day, we celebrate love for others. Commercial interests have turned it into an enormous spectacle. It's the busiest day for florists, and restaurants charge absurd premiums for mediocre prix-fixe menus. Then, the pressure is on to make stellar, earth-shattering love. Yet, there is no day in the calendar year that celebrates love for ourselves.

If you take only one thing away from reading this book, let it be love for yourself. Self-love is that strong foundation that underlies every success story. What you do, what you say, how you think, how you feel, how you work and relate to others—you can trace all of these things back to how much, or how little, you love yourself.

What is self-love, exactly? To help you understand what I'm talking about, I invite you to experience the Sweet Spot Meditation on Love from my Be Your Best Self Workshop. Read this next section slowly. Very slowly. It will take you about five minutes to really settle in and benefit from it. Alternatively, download my Sweet Spot Meditation on Love at www.findyoursweetspot.com, close your eyes, and let my voice guide you through it. As you read or listen to my words, think through and really visualize what I'm asking you to call into your imagination (even as you read, close your eyes for intervals to facilitate the process). Open yourself up and feel the emotions that accompany your thoughts. Resist the urge to rush through this exercise, because this love is critical to finding your sweet spot.

SWEET SPOT CHECK **MEDITATION ON LOVE**

Begin by taking a few deep breaths. Breathe fully, and as you breathe, place your right hand on your heart. Breathe into that connection. Feel the warmth.

Now, call into your mind and your heart the person whom you love the most. (If more than one person fills this description, just pick one for the purpose of this exercise.) Close your eyes for a moment and see this person's face. Notice all the features you know and love so well. The familiar expression. The way he or she is looking back at you. This face is so clear that you can almost touch it. This person is glowing with the warmth and love that you feel, and with the undying belief you have in his or her potential. This love of yours is capable of anything. And you would do anything for this person. Revel in the richness of this feeling.

Feel that love in your heart.

If I could hold a mirror up for you right now, you would see that you are smiling. That's how good this person makes you feel. You are brimming with pride, happiness, energy. You feel connected. You are protective of this person, willing to do everything within your power to shield this person from harm or any form of negativity.

That's love. That's belief, confidence, trust. Feel your heart swell. Recognize the beauty of this person, and your wholehearted acceptance of him or her. Breathe it all in. Love feels good!

Now, for this next part, you might want a box of tissues handy. Ready? With your hand still on your heart, I want you to remember the last time this person let you down. He or she really disappointed you, hurt you even. You were really angry. Furious! Recall your fury, or the hot tears that flowed down your face. How your heart might have broken. How you felt betrayed. You suffered for days, weeks even, maybe longer. Perhaps, even to this day, you still relive fleeting moments of pain. Close your eyes again for a second and feel your anger and hurt.

And yet . . .

This is the same person you summoned when I asked whom you love most. Despite the anger, disappointment, and hurt, you still have tremendous love for this person. You maintain faith in this person's potential.

How? You love him. You love her. Because of that big love, you found forgiveness. You moved on. You stopped beating him or her up in your mind. Your love for this person was so strong, so fundamental to your happiness, that you found a way to pick up the pieces. You rediscovered laughter. You revived warmth. Trust. Connection. You still believe in this person's inherent goodness, talents, strengths. You relish your time together. All of this is possible because you love.

Love is a powerful feeling, isn't it? A few questions for you: To what extent do you extend to yourself that same degree of love? Do you have so much love for yourself that, despite your failures and deepest disappointments in yourself, you can still move on and appreciate your true nature? Do you feel enough love to forgive and not beat yourself up? Do you believe in your ability to take on the next challenge, despite your shortcomings or previous failures? Does your love protect you from the naysayers and the specters of self-doubt?

Unfortunately, to a person in my workshops, it is clear that we have much more love for others than for ourselves. Ninety-nine percent of my clients admit that they would sooner forgive their loved ones than they would forgive themselves; and that they often continue to bash themselves for similar or lesser transgressions.

Love for yourself is the key to finding your sweet spot. Key! But self-love is seldom even a passing thought in our heads. Worse, we equate self-love with self-indulgence and narcissism. Worst of all? We become pretty adept at the opposite—self-loathing, self-doubt, self-flagellation.

Sweet Spot Tip: Remember yourself as a child, an innocent being worthy of the greatest love and care. Consider how deeply that child needed and wanted to be loved and accepted. Imagine encountering your younger self. How would you treat and talk to yourself? Now that you're grown, do you treat yourself with even a fraction of the kindness that you'd show to that child? Just because you're an adult does not mean you don't need and deserve to be loved in a similar way. The only difference is that now, as an adult, you must rely on yourself for much of that daily care and nurturing. Cultivate loving kindness for yourself, and see how this protects you from external negativity.

Self-love isn't just a matter of self-esteem or self-confidence. As you can surmise from our exercise above, it runs much deeper than that. Self-love, just like love for someone else, is an eternal source of warmth, strength, belief, acceptance, and forgiveness. Sure, to attain excellence, we must have a good deal of confidence. But it's not enough. In fact, I've encountered many confident people who don't love themselves sufficiently. For example, a number of my clients are successful executives who are quite confident in their professional skills, but, because of insufficient self-love, are extraordinarily hard on themselves—constantly hammering themselves for minor missteps or for falling short of perfection. Confidence without love's backing is only a shell of itself, brittle and forced.

This love—an innermost feeling that radiates through your whole being—will sustain you through the most challenging parts of your life and carry you over obstacles, no matter how difficult. With my help, begin to build your foundation of self-love right now, and ensure that it supports you before siphoning off all that vital energy to others.

I'll ask you the same question I ask the CEOs I work with: On a scale of 1 to 10, how much love do you have for yourself? Use the following graph to help you quantify what you feel.

1	2	3	4	5	6	7	8	9	10
Disdain									**Love**

You might be interested to know that even some of the most successful people I have coached—CEOs and the like—have scored anywhere from a 3 to a 6. Not one person I have coached has neared a 9 or a 10, despite receiving numerous accolades and enjoying the trappings of success.

Where do you see yourself on this scale? Even if you feel like you're a 9 or a 10, stick with me; you may learn something yet from the rest of this chapter. If you scored lower, what is holding you back from a 9 or a 10? What's keeping you there? Take note, because if you have insufficient love for yourself, you are likely:

- holding yourself back from your potential
- exceedingly hard on yourself
- running on empty, sharing as much love as you can with those around you, but not saving enough to nurture yourself or your own needs
- loath to forgive yourself
- impatient with yourself and with those around you
- judgmental of yourself and of those around you

- prone to making cutting remarks to others to feel better about yourself
- full of self-doubt
- lacking self-esteem or a strong sense of belonging
- dependent on substances (such as alcohol, food, or drugs) and/or compulsive habits (shopping, sex, etc.) to fill an inner void
- struggling with an imbalanced relationship—either giving more than you need to and demanding less than you deserve; or not giving enough because you have so little love in reserve for yourself, and you undervalue what you have to offer
- defensive or paranoid, perceiving even friends or colleagues as adversaries
- sensitive to the imagined negative judgments of random strangers
- overly dependent on external feedback to feel good about yourself
- quick to assume that when someone is being short with you, it's because you somehow deserve it, or because they dislike you
- inclined to let someone else's bad day become your own
- sensitive to unwelcome or unnecessary stress due to any or all of the above

Does any of this push your buttons? It's all par for the course when you have insufficient love for yourself. For example, you might sleep through your alarm and miss your workout. When you finally get up, you berate yourself for your laziness. *Dammit, I'm such an idiot. What the hell is wrong with me? I'll never get my act together!* The day has hardly begun, and you're already beating yourself up. With that kind of morning pep talk, you can imagine how your day will go from there. What starts out as a singular digression (sleeping in) snowballs, and you wind up at the end of the day really abhorring the person that you are, culminating in tears or beers, a container of cookies, a pack of cigarettes, or all of the above. Sound familiar?

But what if you possessed tremendous love for yourself? What if, instead—as you might do for your loved one—you recognize that lie-in as a necessity, as your body's way of telling you that you needed to recharge? Then, as a result, you treat yourself with kid gloves, making healthy, productive choices for the rest of the day. Our problem is we don't love ourselves enough. We are experts at noting all the ways in which we fall short. We hold ourselves back from our dreams. We miss our sweet spots.

I am not suggesting that you develop an overly selfish or self-indulgent attitude. Simply find it in your heart to accept, forgive, protect, and believe in yourself as much as you accept, forgive, protect, and believe in the people you most cherish. With this love, you can pick yourself up and dust yourself off when you disappoint or fail. Nothing can shake your faith in yourself. Imagine what you could accomplish with that kind of self-generated support. That's good mojo. That's the kind of love I'm talking about.

Sweet Spot Tip: Take a look at yourself in a mirror and make an effort to appreciate all that is you. Instead of fixating on your trouble spots, or letting negative thoughts creep in, take in your whole self as a unique human being deserving of love, admiration, forgiveness, and respect. Look past the surface to find that inner spark that lights you up from within. See the potential for excellence. Then, when you are ready, say three things aloud that you love about yourself.

Perhaps you're thinking, *Yeah, yeah, I already love myself.* Listen, of all the people I've ever coached, not one of them has come to me with sufficient self-love. This goes for me, too. Before I found my sweet spot, I was pretty darn good at being self-critical, and if I'm honest, at beating myself up. What a colossal waste of time and energy!

Or perhaps you're thinking, *How am I supposed to love myself when I've despised myself for so long?* Here's my Cultivate Self-Love Sweet Spot Check. It has worked for all kinds of clients, and I'm confident that no matter what your end game is, this exercise will help to set you up for success.

SWEET SPOT CHECK   CULTIVATE SELF-LOVE

Take a moment to answer the following questions. Write your answers down in a notebook or a journal that you can keep for future reference.

- How did you rate yourself on the self-love scale of 1 to 10 (see page 20)? What is keeping you from a 9 or a 10? Begin with where you are now. Ask yourself: What prevents me from really loving or even liking myself? Make a list of the things about you that you find unlovable.
- Then ask someone who loves you to look closely at those self-criticisms and see if, together, you can knock several of them off your list. See if, by viewing them from a different perspective, you can accept them as an integral and beautiful part of you.
- Now make a second list of answers to the following question: What do I love about myself? Be real. This is important! This question will help you get over the humps you've identified in the first list. Consider both character traits ("I am kind and generous." "I have a great sense of humor.") and physical traits ("I have good hair.").
- Now make a third list, answering the following question: What am I really good at? Again, be honest! Think about the general things ("I regularly meet important deadlines." "I listen intently to friends and colleagues." "I make an excellent effort, no matter what the task.") as well as the specific things ("I have excellent PowerPoint

skills." "I am really thoughtful when shopping for gifts.") Write down everything you can think of, great and small.

- As you create the second and third lists, answer yourself in this format: "I love myself because . . . I love myself because . . . I love myself because . . ." Get used to speaking kindly about yourself. If you get blocked, ask yourself what others love about you and then see if you can get into a flow of adding your own reasons.

- Review the second and third lists regularly so that you get comfortable with all the reasons to love yourself and believe in your abilities. Keep these lists readily accessible as handy reminders, and then keep adding to them. As you grow in love for yourself, cross off the items on the first list. Endeavor to make that list as short as possible. Recognize that you have likely spent a lifetime being overly self-critical rather than giving yourself the love and support you need, so be patient with yourself as you cultivate self-love!

How you perceive and feel about yourself deep down inside has everything to do with how you function in the world. The Cultivate Self-Love Sweet Spot Check has helped many of my executive clients turn around their behavior at work. They've become stronger team leaders, earned promotions, and improved relations both in and out of the office. My lifestyle clients are equally astonished at how effective a tool this is. They continue the practice of crossing off and adding items to their lists, keeping these "love lists" in journals or as ever-evolving documents on their computers. Just think of what this Cultivate Self-Love Sweet Spot Check can do for you.

As you come to love yourself, you'll become much less reliant on external feedback. Receiving love from others is, of course, wonderful, but there is nothing as powerful, liberating, and sustaining as self-love. The love you get from others? The icing on the cake! And do you know what the kicker is? When you love yourself, you actually become better at giving and receiving love, making you more lovable all around.

Know Your Worth

Now that we've established the power of self-love, it's time to talk about your worth. Self-worth is a natural outgrowth of self-love. However, even if you're struggling a bit on the love front, you can still cultivate a strong sense of self-worth.

What's your worth? Do you feel that you make meaningful contributions to your work life, your home life, your community, or to certain daily situations, whether subtly or significantly? Do you feel that you belong? When you believe in your own worth, you can walk into any room confidently. Your body language (which we'll discuss in more depth later) inspires others and attracts them to you. Yes, your positive feelings are contagious!

If you have difficulty recognizing your own worth, others will pick up on your ambivalence and treat you accordingly. Think about how you might carry yourself, mistreat yourself, or misrepresent yourself. Here's what you might do if you lack a healthy sense of your own worth:

- Shy away from unfamiliar, challenging, yet potentially fulfilling opportunities.
- Settle for a job that requires only a fraction of your skills and talents.
- Make poor food choices.
- Stay stuck in a bad situation, whether personal or professional.
- Decline fun invitations.
- Avoid exercise.
- Hole yourself up at home, disconnected from family and friends.
- Engage in mindless activities (e.g., watching too much TV, compulsively checking your social media feeds, refreshing your e-mail a hundred times a day).
- Perceive yourself as inferior to others.

- Sacrifice your own safety and comfort for that of others.
- Work unreasonably long hours just to prove that you *are* worth something.
- Compulsively attempt to execute everything perfectly, leaving you exhausted and frustrated; or else slack off because you think your efforts don't matter much anyway.
- Always seek approval from others.
- Defer too quickly to the judgments and abilities of others because you assume they are superior to your own.
- Allow yourself to be mistreated in an intimate relationship.
- Go through the motions without any sense of creativity or passion, leaving you bored, unfulfilled, and underperforming.

Does any of this resonate with you? If so, it's time to ask yourself, *What's my worth?* This is an important question to ponder. If you feel you've got some value, you treat yourself accordingly. You demand respect from others. You make healthy and productive choices for yourself. You take on new tasks with confidence. You make time to nourish your soul. You feed your body and mind with goodness.

My guess is that you *do* add value to the world around you. Your problem may be, as it is for many of my clients, that in the busyness of everyday life, you fail to recognize it. Let me tell you a couple of stories about the effects of low self-worth, and how discovering your worth can change your perspective and make way for excellence, grace, and fulfillment.

My client, Brian, found his life frustrating. He felt he could do no right, so he made little attempt at anything. Brian settled for whatever job his mother hooked up for him and then made the minimum effort, causing him to get laid off twice. Yes, even at the age of thirty-three, he still relied on his mother to make decisions for him. On a personal level, Brian seemed content to stay home, watch TV, and eat junk food. Exercise? Yeah, right. Dating? He wouldn't discuss it. Period.

When we began our work together—I'll be honest here—I found working with Brian difficult. We would work through the challenges, he would commit to his action items (the equivalent of your Sweet Spot Checks), and the following week he would show up having done nada. Brian always offered a multitude of justifications for his inaction. His attitude seemed to be, *What's the point of this anyway? My efforts aren't worth a damn.* After some time, I wasn't quite sure what to do. Despite going through the motions of the coaching process, he seemed committed to remaining stuck in the exact same place. I felt I was banging my head against a wall.

Then, one day, I suggested we evaluate his sense of self-worth. What could Brian point to that made him feel he was making a contribution, whether at home or at work? As was his way, Brian responded with some reticence, but he ultimately recalled experiences he'd had in college, and at one job where his research and writing seemed to make an impact on a larger effort.

Over the next few months, we came up with scenarios where Brian could apply his talents. He then offered to help his boss on a project instead of waiting to be asked. Soon thereafter, Brian realized that his current job offered few such opportunities, so he applied for and obtained another position where he could write.

As Brian began to see his talent being put to good use, he became more motivated, and he finally began to see himself as a full-fledged grown-up. As a result, he began to take on more responsibility and hold himself accountable. With his new sense of value and a new job, he moved out of his parents' house, and now he proudly supports himself.

On the other end of the spectrum, when I first took on a client, Rose, she told me that despite an incredibly rough patch at work (little sleep, lots of stress, and a ninety-five-hour work week), she shied away from incurring a relatively insignificant company expense because she "wasn't worth it." In fact, she made it a habit of passing on expenses that would make her onerous work life tolerable.

The truth is, Rose is extremely valuable to her company, generates significant revenues, and is loved by clients. But she regularly sacrificed comfort, rest, and even her own health and safety to save the company a few dollars.

Sweet Spot Tip: When someone is impatient with you or makes a cutting remark, remember that there may be outside circumstances—perhaps financial or personal—driving his or her interactions with you. Hold on to the value you know you contribute to your environment and recognize that a negative exchange often has nothing to do with you, your inherent worth, or the value of your contributions.

While she delivered excellent work, Rose couldn't appreciate her value and therefore spent an extraordinary amount of time and energy trying to prove it. She consistently worked the hours of two full-time people. She regularly slept a total of three or four hours a night, seldom enjoyed nourishing meals, and constantly catered to the needs of others (her boss, her colleagues, and even her family) at the expense of her own sanity. Rose also avoided opportunities to grow in her career for fear of failing in new areas.

On a personal level, Rose was her own worst enemy. She despised her reflection in the mirror and made little effort to connect with her husband. Physically unhealthy—overweight with high cholesterol and chronic pain—Rose simply resigned herself to living in a constant state of disappointment.

But then, one day, she thought: *I can't take it anymore!* And Rose began to do the work to implement change. She began to identify and embrace her intrinsic worth, and as she did, she experienced a tangible upward trajectory. What was her keystone? The same Cultivate Self-Love Sweet Spot Check you just did (Rose still adds to her love list regularly). Then, by doing the Know Your Worth Sweet Spot Check that follows, she finally came to recognize the value of her contributions to her workplace, as well as in her own home. Instead of fixating on all the ways she fell short and letting that drive her to exhaustion, she found self-sustaining motivation and fulfillment in delivering high-quality work. Rose rescued herself from her old cycle of overworking, overeating, and running on empty.

Rose began to make use of those reasonable company expenses. As a result, she found herself sleeping better, working more efficiently and confidently, and saying no to work that exceeded her bandwidth without fear of devaluing her contributions. Rose has now developed more business on her own in one year than she did in the previous ten. At home, she is no longer subject to the whims of her children or her spouse. She can draw the line where she wasn't able to before.

Rose can breathe again. She is still exploring the power of her sweet spot, but she already enjoys tangible results from recognizing and honoring her worth. Yes, she still occasionally defaults to old habits, and sometimes even questions her worth, but her awareness of those lapses makes it possible for her to step back and do something about it.

Now it's your turn. Ask yourself the following questions in the Know Your Worth Sweet Spot Check to discover and recognize your value.

SWEET SPOT CHECK **KNOW YOUR WORTH**

Write down your answers to the following questions in the same notebook you used for the Cultivate Self-Love Sweet Spot Check, and then embrace the answers. Refer back to the answers often, and keep adding to them as your sense of self-worth grows.

- What positives exist in my life and the lives of others because of me?
- What value do I add to my family's existence?
- How much do I influence the happiness and well-being of my friends?
- To what extent do I take care of myself and my immediate surroundings?

- **How do I positively affect my work environment?**
- **In what ways do I contribute to my community?**
- **How do I contribute to the lives of others, even those I don't know?**

Recognize your value. Know your worth. Strengthen your sweet spot by taking time to understand all that you do to make your home, your work, your community, and even the world a better place. If you find that you contribute more meaningfully to some areas of your life than to others, that's okay. It just means you—like the rest of us—have room for growth. Once you have a core sense of self-worth to work from, the sky is the limit, and excellence awaits!

Drop Your Gavel

We are our harshest critics. We judge ourselves against the highest, often unreachable, standards. What's more, research shows that our brains naturally default to giving space to negative thoughts. As Mihaly Csikszentmihalyi points out in his book, *Flow*, "[W]ith nothing to do, the mind is unable to prevent negative thoughts from elbowing their way to center stage. And unless one learns to control consciousness, the same situation confronts adults" (p. 169). Do you think a judgmental, negative mindset is a good foundation for your sweet spot? Never. Drop your gavel, and instead of combating yourself, combat negativity!

In whatever context I find myself—whether in my coaching practice, at business events, poolside with strangers, catching up with friends, or at my kids' school—I've noticed a commonality among all of us: We judge ourselves too severely for too many things. Our internal voices make cutting remarks, such as:

- "I'm so stupid!"
- "I'm such an idiot!"
- "I am so freaking fat! I'll never look good—ever!"
- "I'm not good enough to get that big promotion."
- "I am the worst mother."
- "I'm no fun. That's why I have no friends."
- "I'm not attractive enough to find a decent man."
- "I lack the skills to find an interesting job."
- "I'm too lazy to turn my life around."
- "I'm so bad. I ate so much junk!"
- "Women don't find me interesting."
- "I am a total failure."

Sound familiar? I hope not, but I know people who regularly say things like this, whether or not they're true. Before I found my sweet spot, I was one of those people. As we judge ourselves, we convince ourselves that our judgments are true. They become unwavering beliefs, which then snowball into negative actions—or, more often, inaction. (We will discuss the power of beliefs further in an upcoming chapter.)

Negative self-talk is a form of self-flagellation. Sticking yourself with ugly, unproductive judgments and monikers crushes your spirit and erodes self-esteem. What do you suppose happens to self-love? Worst of all, as you continue to judge yourself, you become these judgments!

My son, Finn, said something quite sad one day. When he came home from school, he was uncharacteristically ornery, sniping at me, not listening, and purposely aggravating his sister, Sloane. So I said to him, "Finny, what's going on for you today?" His response? "Mommy, today I'm just bad. That's all."

It made me so sad to hear him judge himself like that. Whatever his behavior might be on any given day doesn't change his lovely constitution. He was simply not having a good day, or perhaps he'd even taken a wrong turn or two. But none of it changed the fundamentals of his character. Finn wasn't bad. His actions that day did not define him.

Nor do I believe that you are the bad person your judgments would have you believe you are. You are not inherently bad for the choices or mistakes you make. They are simply choices and mistakes. Don't let them become excuses to give up on yourself completely. If you recognize that you've made a poor choice, chances are you've been punished enough without further self-inflicted judgment, punishment, or labels. Love yourself. Forgive yourself. Learn from your mistakes and pick up where you left off.

Another problem arises when we judge ourselves harshly: We judge others harshly as well. We apply those same impossible standards to others, and are filled with disdain every time they fall short. For example, if we judge others for how they look or act, it's very likely because we judge ourselves in the same way. Our judgments create walls between us and others, leaving little room for empathy or forgiveness.

How many times have you caught yourself judging people you don't know very well in the following manner:

- "She must be totally self-absorbed. Look how put together she is."
- "He's a total snob. He always keeps to himself."
- "I can't believe he just said/did/wore/ate that!"
- "She is so unpleasant. She never smiles."
- "How can he live like that? He must be out of his mind."
- "They are such bad parents!"

It is possible that some of our instincts are correct, but it is more likely that we are too quick to judge. We often have no idea what's going on in a person's life, and yet we judge him or her as if we do. Consider all the negative self-talk that goes on in your mind and imagine how it may manifest to others. How might they be bashing themselves? What good does this do anyone? Use the following Sweet Spot Check to release unnecessary judgments and drop your gavel, with respect to yourself, to others, and even to situations.

SWEET SPOT CHECK **DROP YOUR GAVEL**

When you catch yourself saying something unkind, whether about yourself, about someone else, or about certain situations, step back and really question whether you know that statement is true or whether it's an automatic judgment. Automatic judgments usually show up as absolute statements or negative labels:

- "I'm the worst parent."
- "She's a hopeless case."
- "He's such a jerk."
- "They're so unreliable."
- "That place is only for aggressive banker types."

When you judge yourself, consider how that particular judgment holds you back. Ask yourself whether a statement like that lines up with the values of self-love and self-worth.

When you judge someone else, take the extra step of imagining what it might be like to be that other person. See if you can find empathy and understanding instead of judgment for that character trait or behavior.

And when you judge a situation, analyze whether you're simply dismissing it out of hand and shutting yourself out of a new and interesting experience.

Make a conscious effort to silence the judgment and make room for other, more productive thoughts to influence your day.

Drop your gavel! You'll find that as you ease up on yourself, you'll ease up on others as well. You'll create space for a more positive, open mindset. See how it empowers your life and brings you closer to your community.

Assess Yourself

It's time to ask: *What innate skills and talents do I possess that will help me to live and work in my sweet spot?* What weaknesses or blind spots may be hindering my journey? When I engage with a new client, we conduct certain assessments to develop a good picture of what areas we can capitalize on, what needs significant improvement, and what can be enhanced.

How aware are you of your own behaviors and idiosyncrasies? Most of us go through life blissfully unaware of them because they have long become the norm for us, and generally we don't question the norm. I am amazed—as both a coach and a coachee (yes, I have a coach)—at the power of tunnel vision. This is where the power of assessment comes in.

My favorite tool is the 360° assessment. We begin by coming up with a series of relevant questions to ask people who know the client well. For example, for an executive client, we might draw up questions for her boss, her peers, her direct reports, and sometimes even her spouse and friends—with the aim of collecting honest, objective feedback about the client. Then I delve into several in-depth interviews with these individuals and distill all the information in a comprehensive, anonymous report that I can deliver to my client.

The report averages roughly twelve to fifteen pages, so you can imagine, it's quite illuminating! With the 360°, we glean rarely (if ever) shared insights and observations about the client. We get positive feedback ("Her presentations are always thorough and well written." "He possesses such an ease with clients." "He is such an important and inspiring part of my team."), as well as constructive observations ("She has a distracting habit of picking her fingernails during conference calls." "She must project more when she speaks." "He could stand taller and show more confidence."). The comments are not always easy to hear, but they are certainly helpful.

In addition to the 360°, I also ask the client to carry out a self-assessment with questions such as: What are my areas of strength? In what areas do I have room for improvement? What changes do I want to see in myself? What are my highest priorities? The self-assessment requires time for honest reflection, so that meaningful epiphanies can arise and help to determine your ideal path forward.

Sweet Spot Tip: If you don't want to undertake an assessment alone, go ahead and hire a coach or else partner with a trusted friend to complete a 360°. You can do hers, and she yours, conducting interviews for each other as well as offering your own feedback.

I have seen the 360° work wonders for many clients. Fiona, a slightly aloof top executive, learned how her body language put up barriers between her and her team and realized that her frequent team meetings demotivated the group, instead of keeping them on track. By the same token, Fiona also appreciated hearing how valuable she was to the organization; her colleagues perceived her as the best in class in her industry.

Lester, an extremely diligent leader, realized that his quest to get things done as efficiently as possible made him sound condescending and clipped to his reports and peers. On the positive side, Lester felt terrific about how his fantastic presentations impacted the company's bottom line.

The respondents in Terri's 360° felt empowered to make delicate comments about her body odor and clammy handshake, which sometimes put clients off. But she felt proud that her teammates recognized how her massive efforts over the year and a half she'd been with the company had created significant growth.

In all cases, my clients have been stunned by what they've learned from their 360° reports. Much of the feedback—both the constructive and even the positive comments—would never have seen the light of day otherwise.

> Sweet Spot Tip: That unproductive habit that annoys you in someone else? Consider whether it's something you do as well. Often, we cannot tolerate in others what we dislike about ourselves—even if we don't always recognize this!

My client, Ryan, a dentist with a successful practice, contemplated retirement as he became less fulfilled at work. At the tender age of fifty-six, he thought he might just give it all up to focus on his golf swing. Ryan was bored and couldn't fathom yet another year of the same old routine. However, after completing the self-assessment and our coaching sessions, he determined that he was way too young to pack it in. He also recognized that he possessed some natural talents that had gone unused but that, if applied to another position, could accrue to his and his organization's benefit. Ryan pursued a position to innovate new ideas to improve the practice of dentistry. I received a note from him after his move, and his happiness jumped off the page.

Now it's *your* turn to assess yourself to get crystal clear on your most valuable strengths, assets, and areas of unrealized potential. Check your modesty at the door and take time to reflect honestly on feedback that you've gotten, whether in quarrels with friends or significant others, or through more formal performance reviews at work. How have they indicated you operate or react to situations? What are some positives that you have overlooked?

If you choose to undertake the 360°, choose a willing and thoughtful partner and then use the Sweet Spot Check below to devise open-ended questions that will elicit comprehensive feedback from respondents (i.e., avoid questions that can be answered with a simple yes or no). Remember, the ultimate purpose of these assessments is to help you develop a strong foundation for living in your sweet spot.

Whether you choose the self-assessment, the full-blown 360°, or both, I've designed the following questions to spark insights. It's not necessary for you to answer every single one; simply use the questions to guide your thinking. For the self-assessment, ask yourself the following questions and write your answers down in your notebook. For a 360°, work with your partner and use these concepts to craft questions that will elicit the valuable answers that you are seeking.

SWEET SPOT CHECK **ASSESS YOURSELF**

First, begin with the positive by asking yourself the following questions:
- What am I really good at?
- What talents and aptitudes was I born with?
- What are some skills that seem to come naturally to me— that just flow and make me feel like I'm in the zone?
- What do I do that brings me a sense of fulfillment?
- What do I truly enjoy doing *while* I'm doing it?
- What single act can I execute today that will put me right in my sweet spot?

Next, zero in on areas that may be holding you back:
- What don't I enjoy doing? What seems like a big hassle or obligation?
- What doesn't come easily to me and feels like a limitation?
- Of those limitations, which are real and which are merely perceived as such?
- What do I wish I were better at that may be worth the extra effort?
- What is stopping me from doing what I want to do?
- What is preventing me from taking even the first step toward my goals?
- What unproductive mindset, habits, or behaviors have put me into situations that don't support my growth?

- Are there people in my life who belittle or crush my dreams, perhaps unwittingly? Who are they, and what can I do to diminish their effect on me?
- Do I undermine my own dreams? What can I change so that I support them, instead?

When receiving feedback from your 360° partner:
- Some of what you hear may sting, but be careful not to be defensive, which will only prevent you from hearing and then incorporating any helpful feedback. While you listen, make an effort to keep your body language relaxed and open (e.g., eyes receptive, arms uncrossed) to welcome their words.
- As much as possible, simply listen as you receive feedback and resist the urge to defend your behavior or counterattack. If you can't sit with it in the moment, reflect back on it later when you are calm and composed.

Take this opportunity to assess the full range of your potential. Figure out what specifically gets you closer to your sweet spot. Begin with who you are *today*. This is a step that many of us skip, especially straight out of school. Often, we just take the first job that lands in our laps and let life deliver what it may. Then, lo and behold, ten or twenty years later, we're still in the same job, relationship, or life situation that never fit our sweet spot to begin with. We feel stuck. But it's not too late.

If you're serious about gaining clarity and making changes in your life, assessing yourself is a must. Taking time to evaluate your strengths, weaknesses, likes, and dislikes will elucidate your objectives and dreams as well as help you determine how to pursue them. Let the power of self-knowledge launch your journey to your star (which we will discuss next) and carry you to your sweet spot.

Shape Your Star

Leah is a stay-at-home mom who continually contends with endless responsibilities at home. She has a running list of tasks for herself and for her family. Sometimes she gets them done, and sometimes they just slip her mind and roll over into the next week, and then into the next. Leah is just treading water to stay afloat. At some points, she feels completely overwhelmed by all the paperwork piled up on her desk and the multitude of parenting concerns that she must attend to. It is a rare moment when Leah feels she's attained excellence.

While rushing around focusing on the needs and desires of her family, Leah often loses sight of the bigger picture—of what she would like to achieve or experience and in what manner she would like to do so. In fact, Leah would like to work outside the home, but she hasn't given herself the time or the space to consider her next step. She keeps putting herself off, second-guessing her ability to reenter the workforce and then letting the busyness of her family life elbow her dreams out of the way. Soon enough, another year has passed and she finds herself in exactly the same place she was the year before.

Can you relate? In your day-to-day life, do you keep your ideals and dreams in close sight? Or do you rush around just trying to keep up with everyday demands, or frequently get distracted by things that don't matter much in the long run? It is in these mundane moments that it's all too easy to lose sight of your star.

What do I mean by star? When my daughter, Sloane, was three, she asked me to cut out a star from a piece of construction paper. Without much thought, I grabbed a red sheet and immediately started cutting. I quickly ran out of space for Sloane's star. As I reached for the second and then a third sheet (unproductively thinking, *What's wrong with me that I can't cut out a simple star?*) I realized I needed to have a clear picture of the form, shape, and placement of this star on the paper before I started cutting.

Our lives are the very same way. We need a clear vision of what we want before we chase after it. We need to know where we're going. We also need clear objectives so that we can measure progress. Otherwise, we end up just hacking away, unsure of where we'll end up and getting sidetracked in the process.

Your star is your all-encompassing guide—a map, a blueprint, and an inner compass that guides you on your journey and serves as a constant reminder of how you want to live your life. In addition to your hopes and dreams, your star contains the ideals and standards that will help you meet them. When you take the time to consciously devise your star, you create a plan for the big picture and ensure that the little details serve that vision.

When one of my clients, Sarah, first came to me, she was constantly chasing after herself. Sarah is an executive at a large organization, mother of four kids, and wife of an equally busy executive. As you might imagine, her to-do list constantly grew and morphed in unwieldy ways—mostly to encompass things that she *had* to do, not what she *wanted* to do. Like Leah, she devoted her days to trying to keep up, leaving herself little room to breathe.

When I caught Sarah in a reflective moment, we discovered that the life she wanted was quite different from the life she was living. Here's how Sarah spent most of her days:

- staying up late at night to watch tv while catching up on e-mails she'd missed during the day
- rarely carving out time to connect with her spouse
- frazzled and yelling at her kids to get to bed
- organizing, planning, and carving out activities for her kids while overlooking activities she wanted to pursue for herself
- sleeping in longer than she wanted to in the morning, therefore missing both her workout and breakfast
- gaining weight

Here's how Sarah wanted to live. This was her star:

- connected to her husband
- connected to her kids
- spending time with her girlfriends
- traveling
- exercising
- cooking and eating well
- balancing work with her personal life
- exploring a new career

By allowing herself the opportunity to step back, Sarah was able to rediscover her star. She realized she was so mired in the day-to-day details that she'd lost sight of how she wanted to live. Over the period that we worked together, Sarah became mindful of her star and then, slowly but surely, introduced the activities and the rest she wanted in her days. She and her husband started turning off the TV and having substantive dinnertime conversations, connecting with one another—and not just on the day's logistics. At night, Sarah would get into bed earlier, missing out on nothing but the oft-viewed reruns of *Frasier* and *Friends*.

Now that Sarah was catching more ZZZs and exercising regularly, she had the patience to thoughtfully apply her parenting skills and enjoy her kids more. Now unplugged from the TV, she had more time to reconnect with her friends on a regular basis, rediscovering the camaraderie and fun she craved. In general, she felt more balanced and satisfied with her life, obviating her desire to pursue a new career.

After a few months, the only unattended item on her star was travel. Sarah's family did not have the resources to travel far and wide; nor did their family have the luxury of long vacations. But they started by drawing up a list of places they wanted to see. Then they carved out a fantastic four-day weekend road trip to Washington, D.C.

Sarah rediscovered her star and, bit by bit, she made a conscious effort to manifest it. First she got clear on her vision. Then she took practical steps to make it a reality. It didn't even require her to find more time in her week. She just needed to map it out and then experiment with new and sometimes creative ways of organizing her day.

There were other positive shifts. Her skin improved. Having picked up healthier eating habits, Sarah lost weight. She was more fulfilled on many levels—both at work and at home. Sarah was living her star.

Sweet Spot Tip: It takes time to really picture how you want to live. Make the time. Investing the time to clarify your star shortens the process of executing on the life that you want.

What does your star look like? Have you been hacking away at multiple sheets of paper without clarity on your objectives? Do the following Sweet Spot Check to map it out. Like the Cultivate Self-Love Sweet Spot Check, this one requires focus and some deep digging. If you're not ready for it yet, read on and revisit this exercise later.

SWEET SPOT CHECK   **SHAPE YOUR STAR**

Begin by breaking down your life into its five most important categories. For example: career, parenting, health and fitness, relationships, travel and leisure. Of course, your list might look quite different, but this gives you an idea of how to begin. Just be sure to cover all the major aspects of your life that are important to you, including ones that you aspire to make a part of your life (if you come up with more than five, it may help to write them all down and then determine your top five priorities; or, you can use the Star of David to encompass six). These winners will comprise the five points of your star.

On a large piece of sturdy paper (construction, card stock, or presentation board), map out and draw a star.

For each point of your star, think carefully about how you would like to see that area of your life play out. Ask yourself probing questions to crystallize what these points will look like for you. For example:

- *Career:* What does my career look like? What do I want to accomplish and contribute to my field or work environment?
- *Parenting:* Am I as present for my child(ren) as I'd like to be? How can I fully enjoy my child(ren) and remain loving, patient, and supportive even during tough times? How can I improve the quality of the time that we do get to spend together?
- *Health and Fitness:* What are my goals for my body? What do I need to change to ensure that I eat and exercise in a way that supports my health?
- *Relationship:* What kind of a partner do I want to be? What kind of a relationship do I want to build and be in? How can I create love and special moments every single day?
- *Travel and Leisure:* What trips and leisure activities would I truly enjoy? What new sights, sounds, and experiences would give me a fresh perspective? What hobbies or creative pursuits would help to recharge my battery and put a spring back into my step?

Once you've brainstormed answers to the above questions for each aspect of your life, boil them down to specific priority goals for each. Write those goals clearly on the corresponding point of your star.

In the center of the star, write down your most dearly held strengths, ideals, and values—the ones that you feel will best guide your actions and support you in achieving your goals. For example:

- optimism
- perseverance
- gratitude

45

- compassion
- discipline

Finally, keep this star in a safe, visible place where you can check in with it frequently.

Remember, your star can be whatever *you* want it to be. You choose the five most important points in your life. Certainly these can change from time to time, and you can address the changes whenever you revisit your star. The most important thing is to visualize your star very clearly and always keep it in your sights. Creating a physical diagram of that star will give you something tangible to dream about, work toward, and live up to every day. Focusing on your top priorities plays a starring role in your journey to your sweet spot.

Allocate Your Hours

You now know how powerful you can be when you love yourself, what your star looks like, and what skills and strengths can help you to discover your sweet spot. Here's a reality check, though. Although our perception of time can be quite subjective, when it comes right down to it, there are only twenty-four hours in a day—and even fewer waking hours. Are you allocating enough time each day to your top priorities and goals? I want you to have a concrete sense. Use this Sweet Spot Check to determine whether you are making optimal use of your time or letting it slip away.

 SWEET SPOT CHECK **ALLOCATE YOUR HOURS**

- Identify the three points on your star that are most important to you.
- Take a look at your calendar and tally up the hours that you currently spend each day, week, and even month (whichever bracket of time is most relevant to you) pursuing each of those top three points. For example, if one of the points is feeling connected to your family, tally up the hours that you actually spend with them. Do the same for the other two.
- Now tally up the hours you spend on the other areas of your life—both the remaining points on your star (which are also important to you, if less so) and other ways that you regularly spend your time (e.g., shopping and running errands, surfing the Internet, etc.).
- Now that you have added up the hours you spend on each area of your life and figured out where all the remaining hours go, determine whether there's a disparity between how much you value your top three points and the amount of time you spend on them relative to

other areas of your life. Again, if family is most important but you find that you spend barely an hour of quality time with them each day, while you spend three hours doing something of a much lower priority, there is a clear disparity that needs fixing.

- Carefully scrutinize those sums relative to one another. If it helps to visualize them, make a colored pie chart that represents the percentages of time spent on each area of your life. How can you rejigger your calendar so that it more accurately reflects your priorities? See how you might reduce, or in some cases eliminate, time commitments for lower-priority engagements and thereby *increase* the hours available to you for your top three priorities. Write down all the possibilities.
- Make just one or two adjustments accordingly to your calendar and see how that works for you. Then introduce additional adjustments as you feel ready, until the allocation of your hours truly reflects your top priorities and aligns with your star.

This Allocate Your Hours Sweet Spot Check makes it apparent whether you're actually putting the time in to reach and live your star. Efficient time management can be tricky in our fast-paced modern age, where distraction is the norm, but it becomes a whole lot easier

Sweet Spot Tip: Once you rank your priorities and discover where a disproportionate amount of your time is actually going, be firm with yourself and say no to those activities that fall far down on the list. Remind yourself of the compelling reasons to reallocate your time and focus. What will you accomplish as a result? How good will you feel? Equally, recognize the downside of maintaining the status quo. What will you miss out on? How will it hurt you, your career, or your family?

once we've determined where those elusive hours are going. We may not be able to add hours to our day, but we can certainly reallocate the ones we spend on lesser concerns. Sometimes even a half-hour difference here or there can greatly improve our quality of life and get us closer to our sweet spot.

Sweeten Your Beliefs

Our beliefs, great and small, determine how we perceive the world. We are wired to collect data to support any belief we hold, whether it's objectively true or subjectively concocted. As Michael Shermer asserts in *The Believing Brain*, "What you believe is what you see. The label is the behavior. Theory molds data. Concepts determine perceptions. Belief-dependent realism" (p. 21). In other words, we interpret the reality of our experiences through the prism of our own beliefs. We want our experiences to line up with what we hold in our minds and hearts. Naturally, we want to be right!

I grew up Catholic and believe in God—maybe not in exactly the same way as I was taught in Sunday school, but I still believe. My husband, on the other hand, grew up Jewish, but within the last few years has declared himself an atheist. Once, as we hiked through the most magnificent terrain in Utah, I marveled at God's work. It took my breath away. The beauty of the canyons, the sprawling landscape, the ridged mesas—all of this, to me, was evidence of a higher power. Jay certainly was equally awestruck, but he was blown away by the mystery of science and evolution. That years of erosion and natural events left the earth in this state, with its slot canyons, lined mountains, and multi-ton boulders perched atop thin columns of earth was remarkable to him.

Looking at the exact same evidence, we came to entirely disparate conclusions about its origins to support our wildly divergent but strongly held beliefs. This is how our brains work. We want our experiences to line up with what we believe. We want to be right. This can be incredibly productive *and* terribly counterproductive.

Here's why. Our beliefs, whether we're aware of them or not, influence how we behave, respond, and react in our lives. In one of my favorite books, *Mindset*, Carol S. Dweck, a world-renowned psychologist and Stanford professor, writes: "These may be beliefs we're aware of or unaware of, but they strongly affect what we want and whether we succeed in getting it. . . . Changing people's beliefs—even the simplest beliefs—can have profound effects" (p. ix).

Sweet Spot Tip: Be skeptical about your beliefs, especially the ones that don't consistently serve your best interests. Ask a friend or family member to tell you whether you seem to hold unnecessary or erroneous beliefs, such as "I don't have what it takes to do this," or "I have no time to pursue any of my interests," or "They will never consider me for a promotion." Chances are, your close friends and family members frequently hear you make such statements, even if you're not aware you're saying them. Some of your beliefs may stymie your progress, and a surprising number of them may be just plain wrong.

Consider something as simple as this: Imagine you believe it will rain today. How will that belief cause you to adjust your behavior and attitude as you embark on your day? You will probably arm yourself with an umbrella, slip on a pair of boots or your least favorite shoes, and experience a downshift in your mood. You might even toss your original plans out the window and opt to stay home. Whether or not it ends up raining is beside the point; you've already made your belief a reality. The same goes for any other belief we hold.

Now imagine you have the following types of beliefs: "I am not a loving person and will never find love." "I don't have the skills to start my own business." "I have terrible judgment." "I will never recover from this illness." In any of these cases, you will gather all the evidence you can find from your status quo to prove that you are right. This belief will shape your behavior, limiting your options and stymieing your progress. Unfortunately, and often unbeknownst to us, so many of our beliefs are self-defeating, justifying inertia and stagnation.

On the other hand, if you expose those negative beliefs as the imposters they are and turn them on their heads ("I am capable of loving and being loved." "I could very well start my own business if I

51

put my mind to it." "I've made some poor judgments in the past, but I've learned from them and now have the resources to go forward." "I will recover from this illness."), you *will* find solutions, dramatically improving your outlook and your chances of success.

Take a hard look at your beliefs. Figure out what they are, what drives your perceptions and actions daily. Which ones do you hold dearly, and which hold you hostage to their negativity? Do those beliefs actually serve your higher purpose? Will they help you manifest your star? Do they tap into your sweet spot?

Here are some other commonly held beliefs that throw up roadblocks to progress and excellence. See if any of them sound familiar to you.

- "I am not capable of change."
- "If I change course now, I'll be admitting I was wrong and have been living a lie."
- "I am destined to be alone."
- "A healthy relationship is beyond my reach. I'm too messed up."
- "I'll always be overweight. It's in my genes."
- "I can't run more than one mile without dying."
- "I'm so uncoordinated. I could never keep up with an exercise class."
- "I'm always getting sick."
- "I'll never be able to live without sweets/alcohol/cigarettes/ medications."
- "I don't have enough experience to apply for that job."
- "They like me now, but sooner or later they'll realize I'm an imposter."
- "I don't have the luxury of doing what I want because I need a paycheck."
- "A job is a job. No one loves what they do. That's why we get paid."
- "I can't trust my female colleagues. They are so catty and competitive."

Unproductive beliefs like these run through our heads on autopilot, limiting our actions, triggering negative behavior, and sabotaging our best intentions. Giving life to any of these thoughts significantly curbs productivity and happiness. But it is not enough just to identify unproductive beliefs; we must replace them with supportive ones. Sound easier said than done? Well, perhaps, but it's definitely possible—with baby steps.

Sweet Spot Tip: Even if your unproductive beliefs are firmly entrenched (and have been for years) the simple belief that "change is possible" can shift your mindset and make way for significant change. See if you can embrace that one.

Let me use fitness as an example. Say your goal is to exercise regularly, but your current beliefs are twofold: (1) "I have zero time to work out" and (2) "I despise exercise." What's the probability that you will find the time to work out and actually enjoy it? *Very* low.

What if you flipped those beliefs and started espousing the following thoughts: (1) "I *do* have enough time in my day to exercise. I can be creative in finding the time." and (2) "I *love* what working out could do for me. I can learn to love exercise."

Maybe, you say. Definitely, I say!

When overhauling your beliefs, you don't need to do a 180. In the examples above, note that I didn't suggest you start saying, "I have *tons* of time for exercise" or "I *love* working out." Don't try to kid yourself. Instead, make gradual productive shifts in your thinking. Take baby steps.

If you start modifying your beliefs in this way, you'll start to get creative and find extra pockets of time. You'll begin to look for evidence to prove yourself right: There *are*, in fact, times of the day and week that you hadn't noticed were available. You may not love breaking a sweat today, or even tomorrow, but with this belief you leave yourself open to the possibility! As you experiment, your brain will collect evidence that, in fact, there *are* aspects of exercise that bring you enjoyment. Then, as you get better at it, as your endorphins really start to kick in, you may well find that you love to exercise.

Any meaningful change begins with changing your beliefs, and you can shift almost any belief you have. First, identify what your current beliefs are. Then, step back and see if you can poke holes in them. As you begin to see your beliefs more objectively, you can start to incorporate other ideas into your belief system. Ultimately, these little shifts will allow you measurable room for growth. Use this Sweeten Your Beliefs Sweet Spot Check to start making those shifts and strategic flips:

 SWEET SPOT CHECK   **SWEETEN YOUR BELIEFS**

- Pick a topic around which you feel your belief system needs work—whether it's career, exercise, self-esteem, relationships, or something else.
- Identify and write down your core beliefs around that topic. If it helps, enlist a friend or a colleague to help to identify your beliefs based on the excuses you often give for not doing something that would actually get you closer to your sweet spot. Then simplify those beliefs into a singular overarching one.
- Assess this core belief's productivity. Can you manifest your star and find your sweet spot with this belief as your driver? What evidence are you collecting to keep it alive?
- Imagine hearing someone you care about express this belief. How would you help to liberate him or her from this belief?
- Flip it around so it supports your goals. Again, it need not be the polar opposite of what you currently believe, but use words that open up possibility.

- Write these newly flipped and edited thoughts down in your notebook and revisit them often. Say them to yourself, and start gathering the evidence to bolster them, until they are firm beliefs. Then live your newly refurbished beliefs.
- As you make progress toward your star, and more of your goals seem attainable, continue to edit additional beliefs that have failed you and add to your constellation of sweeter beliefs—making it bigger, brighter, and better!
- Repeat for another topic.

As you sweeten your beliefs and adopt new ones, it may help to create a chart so you can easily see what beliefs support you in specific areas of your life. For example:

Family	I am patient, loving, and understanding.
Career	I am worthy of respect. I am a trusted expert in my field.
Fitness	Working out makes my body even stronger and more beautiful.
Nutrition	Clean, whole foods are delicious, and work wonders for my health.
Fun	I love to laugh. Laughter is essential to my happiness.
Community	I have a wonderful community of friends and associates who want the best for me, and I for them.

Beliefs with benefits! Need I say more?

Detox Your Vocab

The words we use—in thought, speech, and writing—significantly affect the way we perceive our lives. The sweeter our language, the sweeter our beliefs and our life experiences. Think about the following words. Go down the list slowly and read them to yourself one by one. Meanwhile, notice the emotional response that arises from this exercise.

- gratitude
- love
- inspiration
- affection
- progress
- power
- flow
- collaboration
- productivity
- happiness
- sweetness
- kindness
- generosity
- excellence

What's the overall feeling that you associate with these words? Probably a pretty warm and fuzzy one. Now go back and read the same words out loud. Maybe even say them to someone else in the room (yes, your companion may look at you funny, but so what?). Now how do you feel? How does the other person feel? Is either of you smiling?

Now try the same exercise with the following words. Again, read slowly, pausing between each word to let them sink in:

- hate
- impatience
- resentment
- stress
- bitterness
- anger
- anxiety
- disturbance
- fear
- crap
- irritation
- pain
- annoyance

How do you feel now? An entirely different feeling, right? The words we use—in our heads, our speech, our texts, our e-mails, our status updates, and so on—have a tremendous effect on the way we feel and the manner in which we function. Equally important, these words influence our interactions with others.

If you are on Facebook, think about your news feed. Which of your friends constantly posts drivel about traffic, long lines, or starting the morning on the wrong foot? Which of them uses inspired, motivating language? Look at an e-mail that you've written or received. What percent of it focuses on the positives of the day, and what percent is devoted to complaining about mild irritations? When you read these status updates or e-mails, do you experience an uptick in your mood or do you find yourself commiserating by focusing on the negativity of your own day?

Generally speaking, we tend to take care when talking to others. When we speak to our friends, colleagues, and family members, we think before we speak. Although we may have moments of thoughtlessness (particularly with those who are closest and most familiar to us), in general we choose words purposefully, with the intention of being kind, helpful, and informative. We filter through emotions and visceral reactions so that we can appropriately and effectively communicate. Sure, sometimes we are compelled to shout out the first thing that enters our head, but most of the time we edit.

Imagine yourself saying to someone you love, "Boy, you are so dumb. Why do you even try?" or "You're never going to make it! You might as well give up." Unthinkable, right? And yet, how many times during the day do you say such things to yourself? (I know one person who has fallen prey to this. *Me.*) Does that sound like a sweet spot strategy to you?

How do you talk to yourself? I've learned from my clients and from observing my own thoughts that, much of the time, we aren't particularly kind. Sometimes, we are downright mean, and often for no reason. We say deflating and destructive things to ourselves way too often.

In the New York City subways, there's a concept called pre-walking. That means, depending on where you want to exit the subway station, you "pre-walk" to and get on the subway car that will offer the fastest route to your ultimate destination from the second you exit at your stop. New Yorkers are hyper-efficient, and we like to make the most of every single minute.

Case in point: One day, pre-walking my way to what I thought was the best subway car, I turned left when, in fact, I should have turned right. As a result, when I exited the car at my stop, I found myself farther from my designated exit than planned. What did I say to myself? "God, Karen, you are such an *IDIOT!*" (Insert major vitriol here.)

I take the Lord's name in vain *and* I'm an idiot? All because I had to walk an extra ninety seconds to get where I was going? Über-harsh! Fortunately, as soon as I heard those words in my head, I had enough awareness to realize that I, in fact, was *not* an idiot. I pulled myself back and was able to laugh at my gratuitous unkindness for my literal misstep. But there are moments when I don't have a clue how unnecessarily mean I'm being to myself, when I let that inner voice berate me. Again, imagine that person you love most. Would you have called him or her an idiot for taking you ninety seconds out of your way? Not even close. No big deal, right? Have you been as mean (or worse) to yourself for similarly minor transgressions?

If we label ourselves "idiot" or "fat and ugly" or "loser" or "useless"—or even "just mediocre" or "okay"—we subject ourselves to mediocrity and failure. If, on the other hand, we speak kindly to ourselves, if we saturate our everyday language with words that generate positive feelings such as love, confidence, forgiveness, and optimism, we cannot help but create a world of brightness and potential. According to Buddha, "With our thoughts we make the world." Remember what I said about beliefs? Our brains try really hard to collect evidence to sustain our beliefs. What are those beliefs made of? Words! Choose wisely.

In my work, I've heard all kinds of clients—from high school students to chairmen of large companies—say all manner of terrible things about themselves. See if you identify with any of them:

- "I *suck*. I'm not good enough to be here."
- "I'm such a *loser*."
- "I'll *never* be as cool as my peers."
- "I'm so *stupid!*"
- "I'm such a *fat pig*."
- "I *hate* myself."
- "I *hate* everyone around me."
- "I am totally *useless*."
- "I'm a *b*tch*. I can't help it."

I've certainly said similar things to myself, and I'm guessing you probably have too. And most of the time we're not even conscious of how brutal we're being. How will you manifest your star and find your sweet spot using words like those? Where's the love, the support, the forgiveness? Start detoxing your vocab today with this Sweet Spot Check.

SWEET SPOT CHECK **DETOX YOUR VOCAB**

- Make a commitment to notice key words that you routinely hear in your head, in your speech, and even in casual written correspondences. Notice the positively charged words you favor when you're feeling generous as well as the negatively charged words you automatically default to when you're stressed.
- Keep a vocab log (like a food log) and write down those key words every time you hear yourself saying them. Do it for at least three days, or until you feel you have a pretty accurate tally of the key words you use, and with what frequency.
- Now divide those entries into two columns, labeled positive and negative. Do you have more positive or negative entries? Do you see room for growth in the positive column and ways to shorten the negative column?
- Begin to phase out the negative words by banishing the use of the most corrosive ones from your mind and from your immediate environment (or from any environment that you can control). Target the worst offenders first. For example, in my house, "hate" is verboten, and it's incumbent upon my family and me to find other words to express that negative sentiment.
- Every time you catch yourself directing a mean word at yourself, at someone else, or even at a situation, stop to see if it's warranted. The vast majority of time, it will not be.
- Take a deep breath and apologize to yourself or to whomever was the target of your wrath for being overly

harsh. (Remember, we tend to judge others harshly for the same things we cannot tolerate in ourselves. Simply saying you're sorry goes a long way to ease the tension.)

- To help mend the damage, figure out a more caring, productive way to react to the situation. For example, after I lambasted myself for taking a wrong turn in the subway, I might have thought to myself, *Sorry. I didn't mean that. You are not an idiot. You just got disoriented. It happens.*

- If words are not enough, soothe yourself with a kind touch. Something as simple as a hand on your heart will allow you to recalibrate and find core kindness for yourself.

- Practice apologizing and rewording your frustration every time you find yourself using these negatively charged words. Do this again and again until you've internalized just how counterproductive they are and you've phased them out of your vocabulary. The more you practice this Sweet Spot Check, the easier it will be to default to kindness and productivity.

Next up, to further detox your vocab, consider actually talking to yourself—on purpose and with purpose. In a workshop I did with a group of ten women, one participant, Jamie, told the group that since working with me the year prior, she'd adopted a daily morning practice I had recommended. Jamie announced this boldly and proudly, even though the other workshop participants laughed and shot her queer glances from around the table.

Yes, Jamie talks to herself every morning. Before she begins each day, she stands before the mirror, looks herself in the eye, and makes at least one positive statement. Taking the Detox Your Vocab Sweet Spot Check one step further, she consciously chooses to fill her mind and heart with kind, supportive words. She finds that saying them out loud quashes any opportunity for that negative chatter to prevail. On those mornings when it seems almost impossible to find something positive to say, which occasionally happens to all of us, she simply says, "I will find some goodness in my day."

It's all too easy to take on our own negative sentiments or even those of others. Negativity hits us, and we embrace it. We cling to it for dear life and are certain of its truth. As Csikszentmihalyi explains, it's our default—left unchecked, negativity possesses the power to nudge out all else. In *Authentic Happiness*, Martin E. P. Seligman, professor of Positive Psychology at the University of Pennsylvania, writes: "Everyone already has the skills of disputing, and we use them when an external person—a rival for our job, a lover—accuses falsely of some dereliction. . . . When, however, we say the same accusing things to ourselves, we usually fail to dispute them—even though they are often false" (p. 93). That's right. We take as gospel whatever we dish out to ourselves. We don't even evaluate whether any of it makes any sense.

Because our default state is to embrace the negative, it's a much harder, more foreign practice to embrace encouragement, positivity, and kindness. When someone compliments you, do you writhe a bit in discomfort? Do you suspect that your friend or colleague is just buttering you up? Do you deflect with self-deprecating humor? If so, it may have never occurred to you to speak kindly to yourself.

Jamie told us that her morning practice of talking to herself has changed her outlook significantly: "I give kindness and positivity to myself. I don't need it from my boyfriend, my parents, or anyone else. I give it to myself." As a result, Jamie embarks on each day with greater courage and optimism. Instead of clinging to negativity, she lets it roll off her back. Instead of relying on others for positive feedback, she is self-sufficient.

You, too, can start each day on a note of kindness. Even just a minute of positive self-talk can make a huge difference as you begin your day. Figure out what it is you most need to hear, and instead of waiting for someone to say it for you, say it out loud to yourself—with love and conviction.

Sweet Spot Tip: Flip your orientation. Instead of constantly reprimanding yourself with comments such as "Don't screw this up!" or "No more junk food!" approach the same core message from a positive angle. For example: "You'll get this done today!" and "I will make healthy choices throughout the day!"

Finally, a few words to be wary of: "should," "always," and "never."

You might assume there are lot of "shoulds" in this text. "You *should* eat well. You *should* exercise. You *should* detox your vocabulary." After all, a self-help book should be teeming with shoulds, right? In fact, I just counted. Outside this "should" discussion, this book contains exactly six uses of the word, and mostly in the context of telling an anecdote.

Even in daily life, I rarely use "should." Whether I'm talking to myself about how I want to live, work, or be, or if I'm working with a client or encouraging a friend, I avoid "should" at all costs. The word is inert. It lacks any significant call to action. Think about the last time someone said any of the following to you:

- "Hey, you should try this cure."
- "You should start going to bed earlier."
- "You should apply for that program."
- "You shouldn't be seeing that woman."
- "You should think about how that makes me feel."
- "You should always be prepared so you can participate in the conversation."
- "You shouldn't see that doctor."

What was your visceral response? My guess is that you put up your guard, listened skeptically to whatever advice followed "should," and then went about your merry way. Talk to the hand!

Sweet Spot Tip: Notice the words that inspire you. We all have our favorites; a word that resonates with me, such as "joy," may not sound as sweet to you as, say, "bliss." Think about which words you love and make a conscious effort to use them to enrich your lexicon. Notice how this elevates the quality of your life and the lives of those around you. And be guided by that old childhood saying: If you don't have anything nice to say, don't say anything at all—to yourself or anyone else!

"Should" just doesn't work. Rather than motivating, it immediately incites a sense of rebellion. We don't want to do what we *should* do. We want to do what we *want* to do. What we are inspired to do! As one of my professors in the NYU executive coaching program put it: "He should, you should, I should . . . Before you know it, we'll be shoulding all over ourselves!" (Read that sentence out loud for full effect.)

Also watch out for "always" and "never." Use them carefully and sparingly. I notice that my clients frequently use "always" and "never" when describing their own habits and irritations:

- "My boss *never* appreciates my work."
- "I *always* end up getting the short end of the stick."
- "My wife *always* pays attention to the kids, but *never* takes note of what I need."
- "I can *never* do anything the way I want to."
- "He *never* understands because he's always buried in his iPad."
- "You *never* do anything thoughtful for me."
- "I *always* get left out of important meetings."

Note how unproductive these observations are. Chances are, there are many moments in life when these statements are patently false. It can't be that "always" or "never" applies without exception. But in using these adverbs to characterize how life rolls, we dramatically limit our perceptions. If, for example, you think your spouse *never* pays attention to you, you will look for all the evidence to support that assertion and ignore any evidence to the contrary. And what a sorry existence that would be.

Your thoughts and beliefs, and the words you use to formulate them, are powerful keys to your reality. Choose wisely, and unlock the door to your sweet spot!

Practice Gratitude

Gratitude, like love, is a cornerstone of my coaching process. Yes, even with my executive clients, we talk about incorporating a daily gratitude practice. Imagine their initial reactions to that. At first they think it's New Agey, but as they begin to practice gratitude and internalize its power, they quickly buy in.

Why do I insist on a gratitude practice? Because it is extremely effective. Remember, as research has shown, our minds default to the negative. It's so easy to pick apart what's wrong in our lives. But gratitude is the antidote. In *Flourish*, Martin Seligman writes: "When we feel gratitude, we benefit from the pleasant memory of a positive event in our life. Also, when we express our gratitude to others, we strengthen our relationship with them" (p. 30). Who doesn't want that?

If you haven't experimented with a gratitude practice, you're missing out! When we don't make gratitude a regular part of our daily experience, it's all too easy to dwell on how we come up short and how rough life can be. While we're busy fretting about everything that is wrong, we overlook so much of what is good, right, solid, productive, and lucky in our lives. A gratitude practice shifts our focus to what we have *right now*. By focusing on what we appreciate, on those moments of sweetness and excellence that we experience more often than we realize, we can crowd out the negativity and stress. Remember, you can entertain only one conscious thought at a time.

This practice is incredibly powerful. Simple. Free. And if you do it right, it requires no extra time. When I began to practice gratitude, I decided that I would give thanks every time I washed my hands. This way, without taking any time out of my schedule, I would experience moments of gratitude every day, multiple times a day. In the kitchen or in the bathroom, I found so many things to be grateful for. As I scrubbed my hands with soap and water, I would say to myself: "I am grateful for laughter. I am grateful for my new mommy friends. I am grateful that I can sleep at night again. I am grateful that it's not raining. I am grateful for my spin class. I am grateful for my family and even for the chaos that comes with it. I am grateful I'm having a good hair day. I am so grateful for the flexibility of my job." And so on.

This is what I recommend for my workshop participants, and it's what I recommend for you. Once you get accustomed to practicing gratitude every day, it will come more naturally and spontaneously to you.

Sweet Spot Tip: For gratitude bonus points, grab a journal and jot down everything you can think of that you're grateful for. Just follow your stream of consciousness. Use a journal or tap out some lines in a note to yourself on your PDA. This will bring all that is excellent in your life into greater focus. Add to your gratitude journal regularly, and revisit your previous entries when you're feeling less prolific.

One day, I realized just how powerful this practice really was. I am a person who has historically needed positive feedback, acceptance, and love from others. I am, by nature, an extrovert, so I regularly sought out positive energy from others to fuel my happiness. In my solitary moments, it was unusual for me to generate it on my own.

Interestingly, one day in the bathroom, my eyes lowered to my sudsy fingers as I repeated: "I am grateful for . . . I am grateful that . . ." On and on I went, completing each sentence with all kinds of reasons to be grateful. As I finished washing up, I raised my gaze into the mirror.

I was smiling!

I was shocked to find my reflection grinning ear to ear because of the impromptu happiness that gratitude sparked. I had sparked it— *entirely on my own.* An instantaneous megawatt smile. With teeth! And it came from me, no one else. It was in that moment that I first understood the power of gratitude. Massive.

Sweet Spot Tip: The thoughts and feelings you harbor reflect in your face. When you are worried or disappointed, for example, your brow furrows, your forehead wrinkles, and your mouth turns down. When you exude happiness and gratitude for what you have and what is, your forehead relaxes, your eyes sparkle, and your whole face brightens and lifts. Which face do you want to see in the mirror? Which face do you want to be known for? I opt for the latter. Gratitude is a smile that blossoms from within. It enhances your natural beauty—no facelift required!

I know there are times when it is plenty hard—seemingly impossible, even—to find reasons to be grateful, much less feel it. Sometimes it's all just so difficult that stopping to give thanks seems trite and contrived. But those are often the times when gratitude alone can save you.

One client, Paula, shared with me a stellar gratitude experience during a workshop. A finance executive at a top-notch firm in New York City, she was embroiled in a particularly onerous argument with her husband. Both of them hold graduate degrees and are formidable negotiators—uncommonly clever, doggedly persistent, and committed to their positions. Arguments in their home can be strenuous battles to the bitter end.

This particular argument, though, was no run-of-the-mill session. With each contender completely unwilling to yield, the disagreement escalated from a heated discussion to a fierce verbal knock-down, drag-out fight, with stinging personal jabs hurled in both directions. Paula became so intensely angry with her husband that she experienced moments of pure, almost physical, hatred.

But then, in the thick of it, a moment of clarity. Paula realized that despite the profound discontent, the moments of loathing even, the mere fact that she could be having this dispute was a blessing. It was a blessing to be in a relationship in which each member cared enough to stay and fight.

In the middle of the fury, Paula yelled, "Stop! Stop!" Her husband did stop, mostly out of exhaustion. Then she took a deep breath and continued: "I have to tell you that even in *this* moment, I am grateful for you and for the fact that we can feel so strongly for one another!" Paula isn't sure what inspired gratitude at that very moment or how she found the strength and goodness within herself to express it. But she did. Paula's husband was stunned. And they ultimately came to rest.

When you're having a particularly overwhelming day, I know it's hard to see through the mud and feel real gratitude. In those moments, gratitude surely seems like a bunch of New Agey BS. Even remembering that a gratitude practice is at your fingertips? That's a tall order. But here's how it can work: Paula had been practicing gratitude so regularly that even in that unbearable moment, she didn't have to reach very far to find it. As you practice gratitude on a daily basis, multiple times a day, it will come more and more naturally to you. As you experience its soothing, restorative powers, it becomes increasingly accessible. Practicing gratitude is an easy but effective way of flipping your perspective, even during those really tough times. Quite simply, it works. Try it out and see for yourself.

 SWEET SPOT CHECK   **PRACTICE GRATITUDE**

- Pick an activity during which you can express gratitude on a regular basis without taking any extra time (e.g., washing hands, brushing teeth, shaving, washing dishes, etc.). When you are new to this, it helps to begin with short activities, lasting one to three minutes.
- Tell yourself what you are grateful for, in the following manner: "I am grateful for _____." "I am grateful that _____." Keeping going until you have completed your designated activity. If you can only think of a few reasons to be thankful, repeat those reasons over and over until you open up to more reasons.
- As you get the hang of it, experiment with incorporating the gratitude practice into slightly longer activities,

such as commuting to work or walking the dog. Sprinkle moments of gratitude throughout your day.
- Notice the improvement in your perspective, even as you just start out. Then, as you get into the flow of practicing gratitude, notice its tangible impact on your thinking patterns, work performance, and/or relationships.
- Keep increasing the duration and the frequency of your gratitude practice until you become so comfortable with it that you begin to do it naturally and spontaneously throughout your day.

Whether you practice gratitude once a day on a social media post or multiple times a day whenever you wash your hands, the important thing is to incorporate it as a regular part of your daily activities. Practice at least once in front of the mirror with your eyes closed and then notice your expression when you open them; see how dousing yourself with gratitude effects tangible, positive change.

My triple crown is combining the Cultivate Self-Love Sweet Spot Check, the Detox Your Vocab Sweet Spot Check, and the Practice Gratitude Sweet Spot Check. Once you've mastered these, you're pretty unstoppable.

Breathe Here Now

Breath is essential for life. It is sustenance. We breathe to nourish our bodies with oxygen, a nutrient even more vital than food or water. While going for days without food or water is possible, go without breathing for a minute and your brain begins to atrophy.

Breath feeds our ability to think, feel, and move. Breath provides our bodies with purifying energy that rids the body of toxins—emotional and physical. According to Buddhist monk Thich Nhat Hanh, "Feelings come and go like clouds in a windy sky. Conscious breathing is my anchor."

No one had to teach us how to breathe. But unfortunately, as adults, we rarely breathe deeply or efficiently for optimal results. In fact, we rarely focus on our breathing, much less avail ourselves of excellent breathing techniques. Stress routinely shallows and quickens our breaths, shortchanging our bodies of oxygen.

There is plenty of evidence that inadequate access to oxygen damages brain cells, lowers energy levels, causes disease, and triggers myriad health irritations. But what I want to focus on is how it affects your ability to thrive in your sweet spot. In her book, *The Ultimate pH Solution*, Michelle Schoffro Cook says: "Research shows that breathing deeply for even 30 seconds has a substantial effect on acidic stress hormones and, when practiced over time, can have a profound healing effect on mood, energy levels, and cardiovascular and respiratory health" (p. 122–23).

For example, consider what would happen to your respiratory system in the following scenarios:

- You walk into a job interview, and the interviewer immediately starts firing questions at you, aggressively and condescendingly.
- You begin an important presentation on which you've worked diligently, but it's clear that the people around you think your conclusions are totally off the mark.

- Your husband goes on the attack, saying that you never do enough and questioning your daily whereabouts.

What happens? I'll tell you. Your breathing quickens and shallows. Or you hold your breath. Yes, your breath is the first thing to go. With it goes focus, presence, and composure.

We've all experienced this and witnessed it in others. When my client Tina faced difficult situations, she would stop breathing for extended stretches. The moment this happened, her colleagues would know that Tina had lost her mojo. They also knew the meeting would not end well. In fact, because Tina was a senior executive, the people around her also lost focus because they became anxious that she would lash out at someone. They questioned her leadership skills. They stopped breathing, too.

When Tina became aware of her tendency to stop breathing in challenging situations, at first she worried about how she would be able to rectify it. How could she remain in control when it happened? But she had to do something.

Tina implemented the Breathe Here Now Sweet Spot Check. Every night she would practice deepening her breath, evenly and purposefully. Tina became accustomed to the calm, clear feeling that comes with taking in enough oxygen. With practice, it became part of her muscle memory. As she became more adept at conscious breathing before going to sleep, Tina became increasingly skilled at accessing that full and complete breath when she found herself stressed at work. Both she and her colleagues felt the difference.

Dr. Chad Sato is a chiropractor in Honolulu whose approach focuses on conscious breathing. He argues that if you properly take deep breaths that span the entire lung space, the spine moves gently, the way it is designed to, easing physical pain. While Dr. Chad performed his work on me, my breaths deepened and I experienced a sensation of a strong wave flowing from my pelvis all the way up to the tops of my shoulders. I felt relief. The pain with which I'd come to him subsided. Breath can be *that* powerful.

How do you steady your breathing, even when you're backed into a corner? Practice. The idea of practicing an automatic function may sound silly, but, like Tina, you *can* get much better at it and call on its calming, clarifying power during even the most stressful times.

 SWEET SPOT CHECK   **BREATHE HERE NOW**

- Pick a regular time to practice your breathing. An ideal time may be as soon as you get into bed every night, but it can be whenever you have a moment to yourself. As with the gratitude practice, commit to at least one minute at first.
- Lie on your stomach, placing a pillow beneath your abdomen (you know, the part you're especially conscious of when walking down the beach in your bathing suit?).
- Now breathe, slowly and deeply, counting to six with each inhalation. Breathe in so deeply through your nose that you feel your stomach flattening the pillow into your bed. Let that belly go. All the way. No one's watching.
- Then exhale another six seconds thoroughly through your mouth by engaging your diaphragm (that whole area that connects your chest and abdomen) and expelling all the air. Take the extra step of pulling your navel into your spine to expel more. Let *all* that air out.
- Then repeat again and again, inhaling and exhaling deeply and evenly until you get into a relaxing rhythm.
- Then imagine your breath expanding up through your chest and all the way up to your shoulders (that's the tricky part, but that's the wave I felt with Dr. Chad).
- Once you get the hang of it, to further enhance your concentration, match your breathing with a positive meditation. Think of something you want to take in on the inhale and then something you want to release on the

exhale. For example, you can inhale "in with the good" and exhale "out with the toxins."

- I hope you've been breathing deeply and evenly while reading these words. Notice how that makes you feel. Calm, clear, centered. Access this feeling whenever you need it throughout the day.

Practicing deep belly breaths on a pillow on your bed is a great way to start, but you can practice them anywhere—in your car, at your desk, or in the checkout line. Or even continuing now as you read. As you become more skilled and commit the exercise to muscle memory, you'll find that your auto-response of shallow or interrupted breathing in stressful situations will become delayed or even nonexistent. You will feel the difference, and others will too!

Respect Nutrition

Discovering and then living in your sweet spot requires taking a hard look at your nutrition profile. Sound daunting? Agreed. I love a red velvet cupcake, a big sundae (coffee ice cream, no whip, please), or a basket of fries as much as the next guy. But regularly indulging in these processed, fried, sugary foods creates massive obstacles to your sweet spot.

Unhealthy, unclean foods are extremely taxing on your body. First, your body tends to crave larger quantities of low-nutrient foods to allow the essential nutrients to add up. Plus, such foods are often laden with addictive artificial flavors (mostly variations of very salty and very sweet) and textures, compelling you to eat more than you ever would in your right mind. On top of all that, your body must work harder to make sense of the chemically processed substances coming through your system, sapping your energy, causing weight gain, weakening the immune system, and accelerating aging. Who wants any of that? No, thank you.

This sweet spot component is crucial. A healthy diet—like deep, oxygenating breaths—efficiently nourishes your brain and your body. Life can be challenging enough without constantly burdening your body with poor-quality foods.

You might be thinking, *Hey, wait a minute, this isn't a diet book!* No, it's not. It's certainly not about being skinny or fat. My concern is getting the right fuel in your tank to enhance your sweet spot experience. Yes, think of a high-performance car, or even just the most reliable car you've ever owned. You, of course, do the work to keep it running at optimal levels. You give it clean fuel and bring it into the shop for regular inspections. You wouldn't pump kerosene into the tank or spill soda all over those beautiful leather seats, would you?

Now, think of your own body in the same way. As with the car, you want to make sure that your body is running on high-performance fuel, right? For sure! Upgrading to a higher-grade fuel can dramatically improve your performance and your life. I've seen it happen to all kinds of people—including myself.

But every day, many of us feed ourselves the equivalents of kerosene. We make choices based on convenience or emotional impulse, trashing our bodies and our resolves in the process. Fast foods. Too much sugar, salt, grease. Meats treated with hormones and antibiotics. Chemicals, chemicals, chemicals. Then we get sick. We lose energy and motivation. Then we get *really* sick. Think about the prevalence of Type 2 diabetes, heart conditions, cancers, and depression in our society.

Sweet Spot Tip: Be mindful not only of what you put in your mouth, but also of what you put on your skin. Most mainstream lotions, cosmetics, cleansers, and soaps are laden with harsh, processed chemicals that seep through the skin's pores and may have questionable long-term effects on the body. Remember that your skin is your largest living organ, in need of cleansing, hydration, and nourishment as much as the rest of you. Choose high-quality products, preferably organic. Showering in filtered water with the aid of a whole house filter is also an excellent option.

Fact: I grew up eating Spam and continued to do so until I was thirty-three years old. If you're not from Hawaii, the idea of Spam probably repulses you. Perhaps I have lost some credibility by sharing this with you. But I admit it because it is emblematic of the eating habits that I once embraced. From the time I was a child in flip-flops in Honolulu, my attitude was "I can eat anything I want." And I ate everything.

But then, after I gained and then lost the freshman fifteen, my motto became "I can eat anything I want as long as I exercise." I did not care what the nutritional labels said. I just wanted whatever I put in my mouth to be delicious. And oh, the alcohol! Who cared? As long as I burned it off and felt good enough in my bikini, certainly not I.

I disclose these dirty little secrets because many people, even those who know me pretty well, assume I grew up drinking green juices and favoring organic fare. They think that making healthy choices has always come naturally to me. *Nothing* could be further from the truth.

Sweet Spot Tip: Keep a food log. Commit to seven consecutive days of logging everything that you put into your mouth for an honest and accurate picture of your eating habits. The results can be stunning, especially if you tend to snack a lot throughout the day, eat on the go, or enjoy a fully booked social calendar. Simply seeing the foods listed will raise your awareness of your nutrition profile.

No matter what your eating habits are now, you too can ramp up your nutritional intake and start feeling like a professional race car driver in your own body. Believe me, if I did it, you can too! Respecting nutrition is about respecting your body and optimizing your health. It's about energy, vitality, and clarity—all those ingredients that will carry you to your sweet spot. You'll be surprised at how all the benefits of good nutrition keep accruing and accelerating as you stick with it—how negativity slips away, energy levels soar, cholesterol readings drop, moods bloom, and better eating habits stick. When you improve your diet from a nutritional perspective rather than a weight loss one (which can be a losing battle), weight loss comes as a natural bonus.

Here is a challenge for you. Take on this Respect Nutrition Sweet Spot Check. Commit to eating differently for the next twelve days—that's less than two weeks. Take into account any food allergies or other nutritional deficiencies that you may have (if you are unsure about this, I recommend making an appointment for a blood test to find out). These guidelines are an amalgam of tips from several leading nutritionists:

SWEET SPOT CHECK RESPECT NUTRITION

- Make green juices and vegetables the vast majority of what you eat over the next twelve days, while also incorporating fruits and other whole foods. Stock your fridge and pantry with your favorite fresh produce and experiment with types you've never tried before. My friend Natalia Rose, a nutritionist and the author of many books on clean eating, is an impassioned proponent of this approach.

- Clear away any non-wholesome, nonnutritious food items so they don't distract you from this challenge. Keep healthy snacks on hand—both at home and, if applicable, at your workplace—to make healthy snacking easy and convenient. Susan Cross, my friend and a holistic health counselor, advises her clients to carry a Ziploc bag of healthy snacks in their handbags to stave off unplanned visits to the convenience store.

- If you must have meat, enjoy only high-quality (i.e., organic, grass-fed) meats sparingly and coupled with a lot of veggies to avoid added hormones and antibiotics, as well as the naturally secreted stress hormones of factory-farmed animals. (Some health professionals, including Dr. Joseph Mercola, an alternative physician and *New York Times* best-selling author, suggest having a small amount of flesh as a regular part of our diets.)

- Avoid the following foods at all costs: fast foods, processed foods (i.e., anything prepackaged, no matter what the health claims are on the label), processed sugars or sugar substitutes, wheat or white flour, dairy, alcohol, nicotine, or other recreational drugs. (For further information about these dietary prohibitions, consult the work of Dr. Robert O. Young and Shelley Redford Young in *The pH Miracle.*)

You may be thinking, *What am I supposed to eat?* Or worse, *This chick is hard-core. She belongs in a loony bin!* But remember, I've waded through years of junk food, studied scads of nutrition books, and benefited from nutritional coaching. The simplest, most unanimous answer to all of our dietary quandaries is: Eat fresh foods. (Michael Pollan's *Food Rules* is an excellent book that offers clear, concise, compelling information about nutrition and eating habits.) It's not as difficult as you think. The sustainable agriculture movement is on a tear, making healthier, whole food choices more accessible than ever.

I've challenged many workshop participants with this Respect Nutrition Sweet Spot Check, and I have had the toughest New Yorkers scoff at me. One, Jackie, actually said to me, "Honey, I eat my dinner at 10:30 at night. It's fried, and it's delicious. I am *not* doing this." Jackie savored coffee and donuts for breakfast, often skipped lunch, wolfed down a fast food afternoon snack at 4 p.m., and then finished her day with chicken Parmesan at an hour when many folks go to bed. Nope, Jackie had absolutely no intention of taking on this challenge. Honestly, I wondered whether she'd even come back for the remaining two workshop sessions.

In fact, two weeks later, when Jackie showed up at my workshop table, her skin was literally glowing. *Glowing!* I restrained myself from commenting on her transformation because I wanted others to notice on their own. And when they did, they expressed glee and curiosity: "Jackie! You literally look like a different person!" "Jackie! What the heck have you been up to this week?"

Jackie beamed. Despite her adamant declaration that she wouldn't, she had taken on the Respect Nutrition Sweet Spot Check (no meat, even) and could hardly believe the results. Jackie grinned from ear to ear and told the group how energized she felt and how amazed she was that simply changing her food choices could make such a dramatic difference in how she looked and felt. She loved it so much that she even experimented with vegan cooking.

Jackie's experience is not unique. When workshop participants commit to this challenge, they lose weight, gain confidence, and experience an uplift in all areas of their lives. Best of all, they understand how much more they are capable of. It happened for me. It happened for Jackie. And it can happen for you.

Eating is fraught with emotions. Sometimes we eat because we are happy and excited to be with family and friends. Other times we eat because we are upset, sad, or stressed; food brings us momentary comfort. The emotional link is sometimes incredibly hard to fight, and for whatever reason, we find ourselves tucking into tubs of ice cream or gigantic bowls of pasta. The next thing you know, you're thinking, *What's the point of even trying? I'll never have the will power.* When you are feeling this way, get back on track with the Respect Nutrition Sweet Spot Check 2.0.

 SWEET SPOT CHECK   **RESPECT NUTRITION 2.0**

- Instead of categorizing yourself as a "carb addict," a "sweet tooth," or a "junk food junkie," give those labels up and try on some new monikers, such as "veggie diva" or "fresh food fanatic." Free your mind to embrace more nutritious options.

- Remind yourself that your body is your number one ally in finding your sweet spot and achieving excellence. Treat it as such. No one else has the power to do it for you.

- Think about food as vital fuel rather than a pacifier for your emotions. Actually ask yourself, "How will this food nourish my body? Will it give me the energy I need? How will it lift my mood and bring me closer to my sweet spot?"

- When you cave in to an unhealthy craving or make a poor food choice, remember that your food choices don't define you. You're not "bad." You're not "cheating." Detox those judgmental words from your dietary lexicon and be kind to yourself. Make your next meal, whether it's three hours from now or the next morning, your fresh start.

- Indulge infrequently but regularly. Have a cupcake, a bit of candy, or whatever your chosen indulgence is a couple of times a week (fun fact: organic dark chocolate is a common favorite among nutritionists). Or designate one day to eat less carefully. I call this eating "off the map" because it's neutral (there's no "good" or "bad" judgment to it).

- As you start eating more healthily, know that at some point in the future you will indulge again in an "off the map" meal. You're not *forever* depriving yourself of those special treats that bring you joy. You're just reeducating your palate, so it can learn to love more of those foods that are truly nourishing. Reminding yourself that there is more chocolate in your future will help to prevent bingeing.

Here is one of my favorite quotes I once heard a nutritionist say: "If you eat junk, what you think and feel is junk." It makes sense, right? As you go through the Respect Nutrition Sweet Spot Checks, observe your thoughts and feelings. Note what they are when you eat nutritiously. Note what they are when you eat off the map. I'm confident that as you clean up your nutrition, you will feel more beautiful inside and out.

Kate Moss once said, "Nothing tastes as good as skinny feels." I like to put my own positive spin on such mantras. For example, "If you eat healthy, what you think and feel is healthy" and "Healthy feels way better than anything could possibly taste." What is your nutrition mantra?

Move Your Body

Exercise is another fundamental component of the sweet spot strategy. Here are several reasons that exercise is so critically important, most of which you can read about in *Spark* by Dr. John J. Ratey. It:

- grows your brain, making it function at its highest levels;
- strengthens your cardiovascular system;
- increases your capacity to pay attention;
- strengthens and limbers up your brain, just as it does for your muscles;
- triggers your body to secrete hormones such as endorphins, serotonin, dopamine, and norepinephrine, all of which elevate your mood, your motivation, and your ability to focus;
- increases your creativity;
- alleviates stress and reduces anxiety;
- increases confidence and enhances your social life;
- demonstrates to you that you are capable of achieving new levels of mastery;
- improves your health;
- helps you cope with various hormonal changes (especially good for women); and
- slows down the aging process and keeps the brain alert.

Yes, indeed, there are myriad reasons to move your body, including the fact that it makes you feel fantastic. And research keeps telling us there is so much more. Exercise has been called the best anti-aging therapy. If you exercise rigorously enough, it actually produces a rejuvenating human growth hormone (HGH) that literally keeps you young (Ratey, *Spark*, p. 255).

When you exercise and feel good about your body, you exude confidence. Your body becomes an ally, rather than a source of anxiety or physical pain. Listen, every body is different, and every person has different physical needs and limitations, but here's the bottom line: Exercise is good for everybody. *Every body.*

Best of all, when it comes to finding your sweet spot and achieving new levels of excellence, it is also an outstanding tool for breaking through limitations. I have heard so many clients say the following:

- "I could never take a spin class."
- "I am so not a marathon runner."
- "I am hopeless at working out regularly."
- "I could never exercise in front of other people."
- "I will never get addicted to exercise."
- "I am not a morning person. Early workouts are totally out of the question."

And so on and so on. But then I've happily watched them prove themselves wrong. Imagine the power you harness when you achieve a "never" and realize your ability to surpass your expectations.

Personally, I've always despised running. Sure, when I lived in Paris in the early 1990s, I was the lone crazy American regularly (and begrudgingly) doing laps at the Eiffel Tower. I figured it was a necessary evil to fend off the unwelcome effects of the buttery croissants and enormous baguettes I consumed daily. It wasn't until 2010 that I took on the challenge of completing a half marathon.

In training for that half marathon, I remember my friend Ashley saying to me, "I could never do that! I am so impressed!" I assured her that if I could do it, anyone could. She didn't believe me at first, but a few months later, Ashley achieved what she had once deemed impossible. Now Ashley has three half marathons under her belt, each one faster than the last (and all of them faster than mine). She looks amazing, fitter than ever, and she's got this new air of confidence about her. Ashley broke through that self-limiting doubt—that she could never. She did, *and* she's kicking ass!

Labels can be powerful tools here. Think of yourself as an "athlete" or at least an "exerciser." Get yourself geared up with a new pair of sneakers and athletic attire that you'll look forward to wearing. Draw inspiration from your favorite professional athletes, dancers, or fitness gurus. If you internalize exercise as part of your identity, you will get yourself moving and sweating. You will find all the evidence in the world to make it a nonnegotiable part of your day.

Sweet Spot Tip: Walking is a fantastic form of exercise—low impact, and all you need is a pair of comfortable shoes and a stretch of road, a park trail, a beach, or even (as in my case) a big old parking lot! No gym fees or trainer required. Bring your tunes, enjoy the quiet solitude, or walk with a friend whose company and conversation will help you blaze through the minutes.

Do the following Move Your Body Sweet Spot Check and discover how energetic and fit you can feel. Your body is designed to move. Exercise can put you squarely in your sweet spot. And, as my friend Karen Bergreen, a comic and author, has pointed out, "It costs less than Lexapro!"

 SWEET SPOT CHECK **MOVE YOUR BODY**

- Close your eyes and envision how you will look and feel five, ten, or even twenty years from now on your current physical trajectory. Are you healthy and vital, or has time been unkind?
- Now envision how you will look and feel in five, ten, or twenty years *because* you have embraced exercise as a core component of your sweet spot strategy.
- Determine the reasons why exercise is critical to living in your sweet spot. Write down the most compelling

reasons *for you* to exercise and revisit them often to stay motivated. (Sure, you want to rock that bikini or those board shorts, but why else? There are likely far more powerful reasons than that.)

- Choose your favorite types of workout(s)—whether it's walking, running, spinning, swimming, tennis, yoga, dancing, etc. You can choose anything, as long as it gets you moving in a positive way. Don't be afraid to experiment, either. There are so many fantastic options, and trying new activities will keep you engaged. (If you have any preexisting physical conditions, check in with your doctor to make sure your chosen form of exercise is something that you can take on safely and with positive results.)
- Commit to at least two or three days a week to work out, for at least thirty or forty minutes at a time, if not longer. Map it out on your calendar at the most convenient and useful time for you. (Many folks love to work out first thing in the morning; others prefer to exercise in the afternoon or evening. It may take some trial and error to figure out your ideal time slots, but they do exist—so find them!)
- Make exercise a top priority, and find creative ways to make it stick. If due to unforeseen circumstances you have to miss a workout one day, don't just cancel; reschedule it for another day that week. Find an exercise partner. Schedule some sessions with a trainer. Join a class. Have a friend or a coach check in with you each day. Do whatever it takes to stay committed and hold yourself accountable.

It's fun to exercise with people you like, and making it a social activity can be a great motivator. When you commit to a workout buddy, a class, or a team, there's a built-in element of responsibility and accountability—and often a healthy pinch of competition too. Best of all, you become more connected to your community.

My dear friend Farel is the national fitness director for Stroller Strides, a company that gets new moms up and moving and back into shape after pregnancy. A sense of community is one of the most compelling aspects of Stroller Strides that keeps moms coming back. Farel says, "There is a 'village' of support that arises among women who exercise together. It becomes far more than reps and sets. . . . A deeper, more meaningful passion and commitment to their health emerge because of the connections they make with one another. Together they stick to it, and they work harder!"

Also, if you can possibly help it, commit to exercising in the morning. Yes, I know, it's tempting to give in to that extra hour of sleep, but a morning workout is especially effective. Why? First, it wakes you up with a natural boost of energy. Instead of reaching for that latte, you can rely on the extra oxygen coursing through your body. Second, it pumps you up with endorphins and increases serotonin activity, which generates all kinds of happy feelings. Third, getting your sweat on in the morning obviates any temptation or excuse to skip it later in the day.

One of my favorite spinning instructors, Stacey Griffith, has characterized her 6:15 a.m. class as that caffeine boost we need—without the caffeine or the calories. During my early morning spins, sleep rushes from my eyes, and after forty-five minutes of dancing and singing on the bike, I feel happy, pumped, and ready for the day. At 7 a.m. No shots of espresso required.

Every week, confirm your workouts in your daily planner, accounting for any unusual scheduling details, such as meetings or meals with friends. Make sure you book enough time for the workout itself as well as any travel or prep time. Then treat that exercise appointment as you would any other important meeting (avoid canceling, except for emergencies). Make exercise such a regular part of your life that you can't start and finish the day without it—like brushing your teeth or taking a shower, only much more fun!

Sub Out Your Habits

We humans are creatures of habit. Some habits are incredibly productive, allowing us to persevere and achieve excellence. Other habits are incredibly unproductive, becoming entrenched roadblocks to our sweet spots.

Through the course of our lives, we etch grooves into our brain's neural pathways by repeating things over and over again until they become rote. When a thought, action, or pattern becomes so familiar to the brain that it can execute it without conscious thinking, those things become hardwired as automatic functions. "Our hardwiring is more dependable, more able to deliver results, than our everyday consciousness," writes David Rock in *Quiet Leadership* (p. 13). "Our habits are literally unconscious to us; we don't 'have in mind' what we are doing." Habits just happen.

Consider the way you drive to work in the morning, what time you go to bed at night, or the way you react automatically to your mother. Or the foods you reach for when you're stressed. Those aren't conscious thoughts. What are some habits that you have developed over the years that support your growth? What habits hold you back? How have you programmed yourself to behave, respond, and react?

To identify some of your habits, begin with the Sub Out Your Habits Sweet Spot Check, which will walk you through a typical day and get you thinking productively about upgrading your habits. How do your habits affect your choices from waking to bedtime? I've listed sample habits to demonstrate how you might sub out an unproductive one with a productive one. Not all of these choices will resonate with you, but notice which ones *do*. Then come up with your own list of current habits and desired substitutions for each of the key moments of your day.

SWEET SPOT CHECK **SUB OUT YOUR HABITS**

- **Waking.** You (a) hit the snooze button repeatedly for forty-five minutes, or (b) get up and meditate, exercise, or enjoy quiet time to prep for the day.
- **Breakfast.** You (a) skip it entirely, or (b) have a shot of wheatgrass and a tall green juice.
- **Dressing.** You (a) lament the dearth of clothes that fit, or (b) happily choose an outfit that looks *and* feels good on.
- **Leaving.** You walk out of your house and (a) light up a cigarette, or (b) listen to motivating music and give yourself a morning pep talk.
- **Work.** You (a) stand around and gossip, buying into the negativity that surrounds you, or (b) genuinely wish your colleagues a good morning.
- **Lunch.** You (a) take your car for a quick spin through the McDonald's drive-thru, or (b) sit in the sun, enjoying a healthfully prepared meal from home.
- **Commute home.** You (a) succumb to road rage and yell at all the morons who don't have a clue how to drive (who did they con to get their driver's licenses anyway?), or (b) pop in an audiobook that makes even the most brutal traffic bearable.
- **Dinner.** You (a) defrost a frozen pizza and wash it down with soda in five minutes in front of the TV, or (b) enjoy fresh, whole foods and dinnertime conversation with your family or a friend.
- **Bedtime.** You (a) stay up late to watch reruns, or (b) go to bed at a reasonable hour so that you can get seven or eight hours of sleep.

Do you see where your habits kick in and either serve your sweet spot or hold you back from it? At every point during your day, your habits define your choices and therefore determine the quality of your life.

Because habits are incised into our neural networks, creating neural paths that never fully go away, the only way to end an old unproductive habit is to create a new one to take the old one's place. Sure, the old habit may still stand its ground for a while, but gradually the new habit can elbow the old one out and then itself become hardwired (Rock, *Quiet Leadership*, p. 21).

How? Repetition. Substituting a habit takes conscious effort. Because of years of repetition, old patterns—pulling out a cigarette, opting for that fried entree, watching hours of late-night TV, thinking negative thoughts, or even taking on more work than you can reasonably handle—die hard. Imagine digging a maze into your brain with a chisel. Habits run *that* deep.

You can override unconscious habits by *consciously* creating new habits to take their place. You do this by repeating that new habit over and over again to diffuse the power of the ancient carvings. How many repetitions? Actually, it can happen pretty quickly because your brain starts making a new etching the second you start the new behavior. Then, with repetition, the new habit really sinks in.

I've found you can successfully sub out a habit in twenty-one days. That's three weeks—long enough to let the new thought or behavior become hardwired into a habit, but not an unreasonably long time to commit to making the conscious effort. Imagine twenty-one days of:

- consciously defying the snooze button in favor of a little bit of exercise
- consciously reaching for a glass of water instead of a soda, or for deliciously grilled vegetables and sautéed beans instead of the usual burger and fries
- consciously spending the hour before bed reading a book instead of watching reruns

- consciously practicing gratitude at the end of each day instead of complaining about everything that was wrong with it
- consciously saying no to the extra project instead of automatically accepting it, at the expense of your sanity and any hope of a personal life
- consciously taking clean, deep breaths in favor of a cigarette

Twenty-one days. A short time to effect change and create a new habit that will bring you closer to your sweet spot. Think about where you were three weeks ago. Does that seem so long ago? My guess is you can probably remember pretty vividly where you were and what you were doing. It's not such a long period of time.

Just make sure that the new habit motivates you and resonates clearly with your goals. If it doesn't, it will never stick. Your *why* is as important, if not more so, than the actual repetition. The new habit needs your supporting belief and motivation to have a hope of becoming hardwired. Instead of thinking of the exercise as "breaking an old habit" that frustrates your goals, think of it as "creating an exciting new habit" that will help carry you toward excellence.

But don't try to take on more new habits than you can handle at a time. Pick one or two that you are excited to try out. Once you've found success with them, you'll be able to work down your list with greater confidence. In this way, you make your habits your friends!

Choose Your Mantra

How do you approach your days? Do you wake with a spirit of optimism, treating each day like a bright canvas of possibility stretched out before you? Or do you angrily hit the snooze button, whack the sheet back over your head, and go back to sleep? The way you show up in life both reflects its quality and determines its course.

One of my clients, Robert, views *everything* as exceedingly complicated and unpleasant—as if every day were a massive mountain to overcome. He expects difficulty and obstacles at every turn. In addition to carrying his own burdens, Robert also lets himself get bogged down with the challenges and injustices facing others—even those he doesn't know, such as anonymous faces on the news—whether or not he can do anything about it. As a result, with every challenge comes maximum pain, and even wonderful events in life become burdens.

Sweet Spot Tip: When confronted with a passing negative encounter—someone cutting you off on the highway, a cashier being rude, or a depressing story on the news—a simple mantra can protect you from the negativity. Take a deep breath and remind yourself: "This is about something else. This isn't about me." Make the conscious choice to let those moments float away and not ruin your day.

If you look at Robert's life, though, it's actually quite enviable. He lives in a lovely home with delightful children and a supportive (and independently successful) wife. Robert has enough flexibility so that he can regularly see his friends, take solo trips, and pursue extracurricular passions. He continues to forge an upward trajectory at work, enjoying promotion after promotion, each job better and more engaging than the last.

But Robert shows up in his life assuming the worst. And as a result, the worst often happens. With this negative attitude comes no end of stress, stomachaches, headaches, and arguments with his spouse. Even big wins (e.g., job promotions, his children's birthdays and sports events) become unpleasant. When Robert attained a coveted position at his company, besting a couple of formidable competitors, he celebrated for a moment, but quickly shifted to fretting about all of the overwhelming challenges that he imagined would come with the new territory.

Now take my dear friend, Jill. Usually, no matter what the day, she has a smile on her face. Her life isn't easy by any stretch. Currently, Jill is out of work, struggling to pay her rent, and has recently split from her significant other. You would understand if she struggled to get out of bed each day. Jill, however, gets up at the same time every day, goes for her run, and serves her community. She connects with others, offering support to friends and strangers alike. When the difficulties she faces threaten to overwhelm her, instead of surrendering to negativity, Jill instead asks herself, "What am I learning from this, and how will it help me?" Challenges become teachable moments for her—lessons, not burdens.

What do you think the difference is between Robert and Jill? Robert, with his enviable lifestyle, and Jill, with her daily challenges, could not be further from each other in terms of their life circumstances and mindsets.

You could boil it all down to the refrain that keeps looping in their heads. Robert's internal refrain goes something like this: "Life is hard. Nothing is ever easy." This is the tenet that defines his life. Operating according to this negative filter, he shows up for each day ready for battle, assuming and then experiencing the worst.

Jill's refrain, on the other hand, is something like this: "No matter what happens, I have the strength to learn from and overcome whatever comes my way." Through conscious repetition, she has made this an ingrained belief. It is her touchstone, her mantra. She continually reminds herself that, as difficult as life might get, she has the power to dig deep and round up the strength to live and learn.

Remember, your mind can only house one conscious thought at a time. Just as specific word choices and beliefs can help or hurt you, invoking a mantra several times a day can keep you in a productive mindset. When you have a supportive mantra at the ready, you can use it to oust negative thoughts as they occur and allow your day to flow in a positive direction.

What does a mantra look like? The great thing is that a mantra can look like anything you want. It can be a sentence. Three words. A rhyme. A song lyric. One of my client's mantras was a page of positive affirmations that he would read to himself every night before bed, and this truly changed his life. As long as it feels like a natural fit and resonates with you, anything goes! Here are a few examples that I've culled from my coaching practice:

- For exercise: "Committed. Consistent. Caliente!"
- For confidence: "I am strong. I do belong!"
- For healthy eating: "Fabulous fuel. Fit fanny."
- For self-love: "I am full of goodness, gratitude, and grace."
- For parenting: "Loving kindness, patience, and laughter."
- For focus: "I want it. I see it. I got it."

Sweet Spot Tip: Get creative and playful, and don't be afraid to borrow from your favorite song or verse (no copyright enforcers are monitoring your thoughts). If a mantra is catchy and makes you smile, chances are, it will stick and be very effective. *Caliente!*

What internal refrain determines the course of your days? What mantra(s) will serve you best when your back is up against the wall? Do the following Choose Your Mantra Sweet Spot Check to find out.

SPOT CHECK **CHOOSE YOUR MANTRA**

- Take a good, hard look at your attitude. How do you usually approach the day? If you were to boil down all of your self-talk to a single refrain, what would it be? Is it productive or unproductive? Could it serve as a mantra or be retooled to become one? Or is it a negative belief that corrodes your day?

- When you wake up each the morning, check your first thought and make it optimistic about the day ahead. It could be as simple as "It's going to be a beautiful day!" or "How lucky am I to be alive?" (Yes, it may sound contrived, but give these a whirl; when you say it, mean it and then see what happens.) Or it could be more creative: "Rain or shine, *I* will shine today." "I am an artist and today is my canvas." Create a marvelous morning mantra that resonates with you.

- What are the most challenging moments of the day for you? Does meeting with your boss make you nervous? Are you self-conscious in your fitness class? Do you get anxious on dates or at cocktail parties? Does your significant other push your buttons? Do you feel weak around certain foods, especially at a certain point in the afternoon? Design a mantra to gird your strength for each of the most typically difficult moments in your day.

- Write these mantras down and categorize them by their daily contexts. Keep them accessible so that you can pull them up at any time. (I keep mine in the Notes app of my iPhone.)

- Repeat each one over and over again so that you get used to saying it in your head. Develop a rhythm as you say it so that it's fun and easy to say.

- Consciously invoke your mantras upon waking each morning and during your trouble spots for twenty-one

days. With practice and repetition, you will internalize them and become adept at using them effectively.

All of my clients—both my executive clients and my lifestyle clients—have benefited from the power of a personal mantra. One uses a mantra when she gets nervous during presentations. Another relies on his mantra whenever he finds himself losing his cool. One woman strengthens her resolve when she starts doubting her contributions at work. All they do is play one simple line on repeat in their minds and hearts. No one even knows it's happening, but in that moment a well-chosen mantra can make all the difference.

Part III

The Sweet Spot Outside

"My heart gives thanks for empty moments given to dreams, and for thoughtful people who help those dreams come true."

—William S. Braithwaite

Did you find Part II to be hard work? Good news. Part III is much easier. In this section, having found your inner sweet spot, you will apply sweet spot strategies to your interactions with others to help you stay there. Most of the exercises here are very simple and take no extra time, and yet they are extremely effective.

Love What You Do

At the beginning of Part II, I asked you to cultivate love for yourself. Now I am asking you to cultivate love for what you do in the world every day.

In fact, it was this exact idea that inspired my workshops for high-school girls. I wanted them to understand that they could pursue a career and a lifestyle based on what they loved and what they were good at. I wanted them to know that they didn't need to go down a career track just because it was expected of them, or just because the opportunity presented itself. Between law school and working as an attorney, I spent so many years pursuing a career that I didn't love. I only discovered that it was possible to love what I do (and do what I loved) after I left the legal field. I was even stunned to discover that some people love their jobs so much that they'd be willing to do them for free! This turned my initial idea of what it means to be happy and successful completely on its head.

Yes, sometimes it takes a bit more courage to pursue what you *want* to do over what you think you *ought* to do. But the payoff is spectacular. I've seen so many people engage in unproductive behaviors and habits because they are so unhappy with their chosen path. I can recognize this pattern because this used to be me. When we don't find consistent joy and fulfillment in how we spend the majority of our day, we tend to seek happiness elsewhere. The problem is, by the end of the day, we're usually too tapped out to reach for anything more than a quick fix—whether in the form of food, alcohol, drugs, sex, shopping, or TV. The only way out of this cycle is to take an honest look at your main occupation.

What's the one thing in your life that takes up most of your waking hours? Your career? Taking care of your family? Social commitments? Charity work? If you love this one pervasive aspect of your life, you really rock your sweet spot.

I once attended a conference in Washington, D.C., for nonprofit organizations that won grants from the federal government to provide survivors of sexual assault with needed services. I overheard one table of attendees talking about the commutes they endured for their jobs. Many of them complained, but one person who drove two and a half hours each way told the others: "It's easy. I do it because I love what I do. I could never bear the commute if I didn't love my job." When you truly love what you do, other aspects of your life have a way of falling into place.

My client, Meredith, agonized over her next career step. A highly esteemed leader, Meredith was ready to take on a different industry and work environment, so she entertained a potential offer from a consumer brand. They were willing to do whatever it took to get her. For Meredith, the company's solid reputation and generous offer were attractive, but she knew she wouldn't love working within its traditional structure. Despite this knowledge and a keen desire to start something on her own, she kept this "safe option" active for months, visiting, and revisiting, the company's headquarters for continued discussions.

In the end, Meredith was honest with herself and chose to walk away. Even though it was scarier, she pursued the more entrepreneurial route. Within a year, she has built out a company with interesting and far-reaching projects. Now, working in her sweet spot, Meredith absolutely loves what she's doing, and she isn't looking back. She laughs when asked about that other opportunity. Like Meredith did, look before you leap. Give yourself some time to consider carefully what you love to do and what your next step will be. Surely, it can be tempting to take what's right in front of you, but it may not always the right choice.

My dear friend Jake spent eight years pouring his energy and expertise into building out a lifestyle company in New York City. Most of the time, he was in his element—happily working twelve-hour days without flinching. Unfortunately, toward the end of his time there, Jake spent larger chunks of his day executing tasks that didn't align with his star. On top of that, he found himself stressed and burnt out from the long hours.

Jake's normally sunny disposition began to seem forced. After some hand-wringing (he still loved his team of colleagues), Jake opted out so that he could revitalize. He left this job he'd loved for so long to return to helping clients to heal their injuries. Within a month, Jake revived his own health and fitness schedule and began cooking and eating well again. In that month, he lost inches around his waist and his infectious smile returned.

Jake is a walking example of how loving what you do makes an enormous difference. At the end of his time at his previous job, he enjoyed some opportunities to work one-on-one with his clients, but so many other administrative tasks that he did not enjoy figured into the equation and took him out of his sweet spot. Now, Jake's daily tasks involve primarily working with clients, which he loves. He is healthy, and his business is soaring!

 SWEET SPOT CHECK **LOVE WHAT YOU DO**

- **Revisit the Assess Yourself Sweet Spot Check (page 39). Take stock of where you are now versus where you want to be. Are you in a position that you love and that you're good at? Or do you struggle just to make it through the day?**
- **Has your job description or main occupation changed? If so, what has changed for better or for worse? Are you**

doing more or less of what you enjoy? What might be an opportunity for growth and fulfillment in your current situation?

- If your job description or main occupation hasn't changed in quite some time, are you comfortable with that? Or how might your skills and level of engagement have stagnated as a result?
- What are some ways to shift your perspective so you can appreciate all the goodness in your current situation?
- If you can't change what you do every day (e.g., you must take care of your family), what elements can you add or subtract to boost genuine enjoyment and invigorate the love? For example, it may be as simple as taking on a little bit of volunteer work for a cause that is particularly meaningful to you or incorporating one activity that you love, such as yoga or creative writing. To subtract, you might delegate an essential task that you dislike doing or recognize that some things are just nonessential. Or you could simply add a shot of gratitude throughout the day.
- If you can't shift your perspective or bring some revitalizing changes to your job description, revisit your Assess Yourself Sweet Spot Check (page 39) and see what kind of position you would love.

Many of my clients come to me when they no longer love what they do, if they ever did to begin with. My job is not to immediately dismantle their lives and throw the baby out with the bathwater. First, I start with an examination of what they love—in themselves, and then in what they do in their daily lives. Sometimes finding the love is just a matter of shifting perspectives, making small but vital adjustments, and appreciating the goodness (or the potential for it) that's already inherent in their current situation. Other times, it does require more drastic measures—a career change, a relationship change, something quite new. But with all of them, we begin with finding the love—the sweetness—where it already exists and building from there. Use Meredith's and Jake's stories as inspiration. Pursue what you love and reclaim your sweet spot.

Celebrate Your Wins–Big and Little

Growing up, how much positive feedback and encouragement did you get from your parents and elders? Even if you had an imperfect childhood, you probably received quite a lot, whether it was when you brought home an art project from school, or the first time you rode a bike, or that time you rocked the spelling bee. Or even when you tried and failed at something:

- "It's okay, honey. There's always next time."
- "You did a great job!"
- "I know your effort will really pay off."
- "I love the way you keep getting up when you fall down!"

The problem is that, as adults, *we* are our first line of feedback, and we tend to talk to ourselves in the opposite way. Our own feedback is largely negative and discouraging:

- "I am such a loser."
- "I totally screwed that up. No surprise."
- "He didn't like me. No second date, as usual."
- "I could *never* do something like that!"
- "I'm just a glass-half-empty type."

As children, we drink in the positive reinforcement of our elders and learn to believe in ourselves. But as life progresses and those encouraging voices fall away, we start second-guessing ourselves and comparing ourselves to others. (That damn bell curve!) We begin to agonize about all the ways we come up short, forgetting to give ourselves credit along the way. We don't celebrate our wins, big or little. Before we know it, we have strayed far, far away from our sweet spot.

My friend Morgan is a beautiful, talented, and hilarious woman who, if you met her, you'd want among your best friends. For years, though, she battled an extremely tough eating disorder and a negative body image. For almost two decades, these issues dominated her life. Morgan called herself terrible (horrifying!) names as she binged and purged daily.

Finally, when she'd had enough, she undertook intense physical and emotional work to heal herself. After years of healing, Morgan broke the cycle, enjoyed genuine confidence, and developed a true appreciation for who she was. Despite these major leaps forward, however, Morgan sometimes became incredibly impatient with her progress and relapsed, returning to late-night binging (but, fortunately, not purging). Nonetheless, even in dire moments, Morgan no longer resorted to depressing labels. She still possessed a great deal of genuine self-love and recognized that she could continue her important work to stay healthy. But when she relapsed, the disappointment was there and very real for Morgan.

To help her cope with the disappointment on one particularly difficult day, I suggested to Morgan that she flip the situation around and look at it from another vantage point. Instead of beating herself up for resorting to her old behavior, she could *celebrate* the new, productive behaviors that made her feel good. After all, she had journeyed a long way from the life she had once led. Progress! Even with the intermittent backslide, she was still winning the battle. Now, Morgan celebrates her "wins," big and little. Instead of admitting defeat at a bump in the road, Morgan picks herself up and gathers the support she needs to move forward. She celebrates her victories and learns from her missteps.

Are you still unclear about what you can celebrate? Well, there are the obvious big wins that you'd naturally want to celebrate after the long journey of getting there. To give you an idea of the range of possibilities, here are some achievements that have qualified as big wins for my clients:

- a big job promotion
- losing ten pounds

- a healthy doctor's report after a health scare
- a new baby
- a college acceptance
- launching a business
- running a long race
- finishing a painting
- delivering a well-prepared speech

Equally, though, I want you to let yourself feel a sense of achievement over smaller (even much smaller) wins. These are the little achievements that fuel your motivation every single day and keep you grooving in your sweet spot. Again, drawing from some of my clients' experiences, here are some examples of how you might celebrate little wins:

- Revel in your ability to breathe through a difficult situation.
- Congratulate yourself for getting out of bed this morning.
- Feel good about detoxing even one unproductive word from your vocabulary.
- Pat yourself on the back for actually attending that networking event.
- Smile at your ability to meditate for two minutes.
- High-five yourself for having a glass of water instead of that cigarette.
- Admire your restraint around the cookie jar.
- Praise yourself for not losing your cool in traffic.
- Applaud yourself for choosing to take the stairs over the elevator.
- Hug yourself for spending the evening with a book instead of watching TV.

When I encourage you or my clients to celebrate wins, big and little, I am also envisioning actual celebrations. For example, there's the celebratory party or drinks with friends, which will enhance your achievement with positive feelings all around. But remember to celebrate smaller wins actively, too. For example, depending on the occasion, you might:

- Dance around to your favorite tune in your office or living room.
- Give someone a bear hug.
- Call a friend to share the good news.
- Reward yourself with that treat you've been eyeing.
- Go for a walk or a hike, or enjoy another activity that makes you feel great.
- Watch that movie you've been wanting to see.

Celebration can take any form, as long as it more or less fits the occasion and makes you feel good. Just remember to make the time for it.

Do you celebrate your wins? How do *you* do it? What achievements, big or little, can you cheer about on your journey to your star? Get out your journal and do the following Celebrate Your Wins Sweet Spot Check to find out.

 SWEET SPOT CHECK   **CELEBRATE YOUR WINS**

- **Focus on the present moment. What is good about right now?**
- **Notice what's worked. What have you done that's enabled you to get to where you are right now?**
- **Contrast where you are today versus where you were a year ago. What can you identify that's better right now?**
- **Contrast where you are today versus where you were six months ago. What do you feel is better right now?**
- **Contrast where you are today versus where you were only a week ago. Can you identify anything that's better right now?**

- Recall a challenge—whether personal or professional, big or small—that you pulled through even just yesterday. How proud do you feel of yourself?
- What is something you've done today—as insignificant as it may seem—that made you or someone else feel good? Did you exercise a bit of self-control with that dessert? Did you hold the door open for a stranger? Recognize even the smallest actions.
- Take stock of all the positive steps you've just identified. For all of the above, give yourself a pat on the back or even celebrate in a more substantial way. Sit back and take a deep breath to inhale the progress that you've made.

Give yourself the gift of positive feedback in the same way you would praise and encourage a five-year-old learning to tie his shoe. Celebrate both the effort and the achievement! Some wins may seem insignificant in the greater context of your life, but it's the little wins that can keep you going and shift you to a positive perspective. No matter how bad your day might get, there's always *something* to celebrate.

Keep a Positive Tally

Yes, even more than just the occasional pat on the back, or celebrating your wins over the course of a long period, keeping a positive tally throughout any given day can keep you flowing in your sweet spot. As you celebrate your little wins, make an effort to aggregate them each day into a powerful positive tally.

Have you ever had one of those days? You overslept—again. Your clothes are *so* not hip, and none of them fit right. Your job sucks. Your presentation bombed. You're getting wrinkles *and* zits at the same time. You caved to the vending machine when you swore you were going to be "good" today. Your kids scream, "You are the worst mom *ever!*" Your husband is late, as usual. Unbelievable. What's the tally? A pretty negative one. And it was all too easy to make that happen. How do you protect yourself from that?

So many of my clients, no matter how successful or accomplished, are prone to days like this—where they pile on the negativity and descend into self-pity, pessimism, and defeatism. Once you start recognizing all the little negative elements of your day, it's easy to add them all up and just say, "Ugh, I'm having such a bad day!"—even if it's only 7:30 in the morning.

At one of my workshops, Elle lamented that she'd been feeling this overwhelming sense of futility. So many things were wrong with her personal and professional life: a bad breakup, a job layoff, an unclear path with a new company. Elle felt like she was drowning. Her positive tally was nonexistent, but her negative tally, boy, that was a coffee table book!

I asked Elle to do a number of things to find her positive tally, warning her that it would require some conscious effort. Now I ask the same of you in the following Sweet Spot Check. Keep a mental tally as you journey through your day, or else tally it all up in writing at the end of each day so you can note your progress.

SPOT CHECK **KEEP A POSITIVE TALLY**

- Embrace the present moment: What's good about *right now*? (Notice this is how we kicked off the Celebrate Your Wins Sweet Spot Check.) What can you be grateful for right now?
- Embrace the day: What do you like about today? Look around, observe, listen. Take in your surroundings and focus on what the day has to offer.
- Embrace yourself: What do you appreciate about yourself today? What have you done or said that has brought some element of goodness to yourself and/or to others?
- Embrace other people: What have you liked about your interactions with others today? For example, you might have noticed the polite smile of a stranger or appreciated a genuine hug from a friend. What have the people around you said or done to bring some element of goodness to your day? What wins have you celebrated with others? Have they shared any with you?
- Flip the negative tally: Resist the urge to chalk up one or two bad things to just having a horrible day. Instead, look at them as aberrations. Better yet, if possible, find a simple way to flip or at least neutralize that negative with a positive.

You'll notice that this Keep a Positive Tally Sweet Spot Check is simply a matter of aggregating all the goodness we've discussed in previous chapters within the framework of a single day. Tally up the goodness in your life by doing it every single day, rather than letting your brain default to a negative tally with the first aggravation.

Unplug and Reconnect

A few years ago, I attended a seminar that changed my life. At the eight-day Hoffman Process in California, I learned so much about myself and was able to effect profound perceptual changes that have improved my life a thousandfold. As a bonus, I made new meaningful friendships that I've been cultivating ever since.

But one of the rules of the Hoffman Process stuck out like a huge sore thumb: No telephone or e-mail access for eight days. *Eight* days. There were other rules, too. No alcohol. No sex. No TV. No music. No exercise. No masturbation. *Those* I could handle for eight days. But no iPhone? No connection to the world? How in God's name would I survive?

I understand the purpose now. We are so connected to things outside us—people, media, TV, radio, shopping, food, etc.—that we lose connection with ourselves. We, as Hoffman says, "numb out" by relying on external sources to keep us entertained and fulfilled.

For eight days, I found myself wide awake at 4:30 or 5:00 a.m. with nothing to do but be with my own thoughts and feelings. No Facebook. No texts. No reaching out to someone in a different time zone. No newspaper. No book. No TV. No Jay. No Sloane and Finn. I had no choice but to check in and see how I was feeling. *Scary!*

At first, it was weird. I realized then that I was *constantly* connected to the external world. I would make myself busy at all hours of the day to feel productive. Sure, in a way, this was good because I would get things done. Then again, if I was just doing it compulsively—how productive was I being, really? Wasn't I just making myself busy?

As the eight days progressed, I got comfortable with the quiet. I reflected on thoughts and feelings that I would have otherwise ignored. I took more time to feel real gratitude. Without feeling rushed or overwhelmed by so much extraneous stuff, I was able to nourish my body and soul. At first I thought I might actually die without the external connection, but by midweek I found myself really enjoying the freedom.

What a relief! Being unplugged gave way to inward connection and illuminated how much I was missing out on in life by being so occupied. I made a vow to be more present—to listen to myself, to enjoy my kids, and to really be with my husband. After completing the eight days without electronics, I found myself much more open to my thoughts and to the beauty of the city I lived in, rather than constantly multitasking with phone calls and e-mails while rushing from one appointment to another.

You don't have to unplug for eight days like I did. If, however, you depend heavily on your electronic gadgets to get through the day, I recommend doing the following Sweet Spot Check. It's a great way to reconnect with yourself and with the people who share your physical space.

 SWEET SPOT CHECK   **UNPLUG AND RECONNECT**

- Make a habit of setting your phone and computer aside and turning the TV or music off for short periods of time, once or twice a day. Choose times when you would ordinarily rely on your electronics for entertainment or distraction, such as while eating lunch at your desk or driving to the store. Make friends with the quiet. Use that time to check in with yourself. Observe your thoughts, your feelings, your breathing.

- As you become more accustomed to the quiet, make those periods longer. Carve out a "no electronics" zone. During dinner or before bedtime are excellent choices. Make this a sacred time when you are fully present with yourself and, if applicable, with those who share your physical space. Use this as an opportunity to reconnect with yourself and make your interactions with others more meaningful.

- Resist the urge to talk on your phone or text while walking (and certainly while driving). Instead, notice your surroundings—the sights, the sounds, the smells, the air. Use all of your senses to appreciate the physical world around you. Breathe deeply.
- Become a good listener. Make a conscious effort to listen with undivided attention—to your own thoughts and to those of others. Really listen, not just to the words but also to the emotions behind them. (It's impossible to be a good listener if you're wondering who's calling or texting you. Unless you're expecting a really important message, be courteous and silence your phone.)

After putting the kids to bed most nights, my husband and I sit at the kitchen table. No TV, no music, and certainly no PDAs. Whether it's for five minutes or for a couple of hours, it has become a ritual that we can look forward to each night. The absence of distracting pings or background noise allows for meaningful and deep conversation. We have enjoyed the best connections during these kitchen table conversations where it's just the two of us.

Sweet Spot Tip: If you have a hard time quieting your mind during the "no electronics" periods of your day, focus on your gratitude practice, do a deep breathing exercise, or just repeat one of your mantras to yourself. You'll find that this time allows you to reconnect with yourself and with the positivity in your life. You may also use this time just to be with friends or family.

Try it. Leave your Blackberry at home. Turn off the TV. Even your iPod. Get comfortable with the quiet, whether on your own or with someone you love. Find a comfortable place to sit. Go for a walk with no specific destination. Unplugging from the external chatter even for short periods can make a big difference in your day. See what you have to say to yourself. See what you have to say to that important person sitting across from you.

You'll find that as your connection with yourself deepens, you'll get better at giving your full attention to the people around you. I promise. You'll listen more carefully, communicate more effectively, and you'll show more affection. Disconnect to reconnect, and experience the excellence!

Make the Technology Connection

Yes, I know I just encouraged you to unplug, but by the same token, you can use technology in beneficial ways. Certainly, technology consumes a lot of our time, energy, and, often, patience, but it also provides wonderful ways to streamline our lives, maintain long-distance friendships, and reconnect with old acquaintances.

Once a month, together with eight other women, I meet with Dr. Sandra Mann, a brilliant parenting and early childhood development expert with a practice in New York City. She warns us against the evils of technology and screen time for our kids. Diminishes creativity! Interrupts connection! Deadens brain cells! Puts life on display in a fish bowl! Weakens social skills! Causes frequent miscommunication! For sure. I'd say this is true of children and adults alike.

However, since technology is an unavoidable part of modern life, I'd like to take some time to focus on the upside of technology and how it can help you find your sweet spot.

First, there's the electronic calendar. Check out the basic calendar on your Mac, PC, or e-mail account. I love this feature of my Mac. I can color-code my calendar entries for each person in my family, so that I can see who's where and for how long at any given time. I also preschedule regular appointments to keep myself on track. Meetings. Exercise. Meditation. Conference calls. Family time. Date nights. Important phone calls. I can also sync my calendar with others' so that the whole family or office is connected and coordinated! I use my electronic calendar to help streamline my administrative tasks and allocate more time for what I love. If you haven't fully explored the wonders of the electronic calendar, I highly recommend you do. Deploy this technology regularly to make the most efficient, productive, and meaningful use of your time!

Second, your iPhone or other handheld device can be a source of inspiration, as I learned from my dear friend Lisa. There's a wonderful alarm feature on the iPhone that lets you include a wake-up message. Imagine waking up to an inspirational message on your alarm clock: "Here's the start to another beautiful day!" Or "Our truest life is when we are in dreams awake." Or "To love oneself is the beginning of a lifelong romance."

You need not limit these messages to your morning wake-up call. Lisa sets multiple reminders throughout the day. In fact, when we were sitting at dinner one night gabbing about all things essential and nonessential, her alarm went off, and she showed me an inspirational quote that brought us both back to what was important. And when her family stayed with ours one long weekend, her alarm went off a couple of times, each time with a different encouragement. One, simply: "Smile!" For Lisa, these inspirational messages help, particularly at the end of the day, when she's contending with four kids, dirty laundry, and dinner prep. Sometimes she just needs a reminder to step back, take a breath, and smile.

Third, the ubiquitous password. How many times a day do you type in a password to access your phone, e-mail, or the various accounts and websites you visit? Countless! Activate these passwords as sources of frequent inspiration. They can be so much more than just passive arrangements of letters and numbers. Pick passwords that inspire and motivate you. Let them remind you of what's important.

Here, I'll give you some examples. Imagine typing any of the following words in combination with your favorite number about fifty times a day:

- Love13
- Happiness88
- 7Passion
- Patience3
- Bliss44
- Calming9
- 100DeepBreaths

115

- Relaxation101
- Kindness33
- Compassion12

Pick words that make you feel good, calm, and inspired. They can be feelings, values, or characteristics to which you aspire. The mere act of typing these words on this page made me breathe more deeply and feel a sense of calm. To help stay positive and inspired through-out my days, I have chosen a number of passwords that connote joy, fun, passion, and patience. Several times a day, as I tap them into my iPhone, e-mail, and fitness class log-ins, I experience an uptick in my mood. This strategy helps me immeasurably as I am reminded (even if only for a second) of the word's meaning and its place in my life.

Finally, if you're trying to lose weight, keep to an exercise pro-gram, cultivate a more positive attitude, or achieve pretty much any-thing else, there are gadgets, apps, and websites that will keep you honest. Find one that works for you, whether it's for counting calories or logging your walks. Three of my favorites: UP by Jawbone, Map My Walk, and Feeling Now. The first gadget tracks how you sleep, move, feel, and eat; the second app tracks your walks or runs; and the third app tracks your thoughts and feelings at any given point. Search for the websites and smart-phone apps that will best serve your goals.

As long as technology is a normal part of your life, utilize it to help you manifest your star and live in your sweet spot.

 SWEET SPOT CHECK **MAKE THE TECHNOLOGY CONNECTION**

- If you have a computer or e-mail account, chances are you have an electronic calendar. Locate it and start put-ting it to use. Explore its various features. Find ways to cluster and streamline your daily obligations so you can allocate more time to what's important to you. Align the contents of your calendar with your star.

- **Find inspiration in your daily wake-up calls, and during those other points in the day when you need a boost. Use Lisa's trick of injecting bursts of positivity throughout the day by sending yourself inspiring reminders when you'll most likely need them. Choose mantras, quotes, or messages that will revive your spirit.**
- **Upgrade your electronic passwords to frequently accessed accounts and websites. Choose words and numbers that inspire you personally.**
- **Find websites and apps that will best serve your specific goals. Whether you are trying to lose weight, get fit, learn a new skill, or something else, there are many electronic resources available to you. Explore. Experiment. Have fun with it. (But be discerning, lest you create more electronic clutter than necessary!)**

Making technology work for you is one of those sweet spot strategies that requires minimal input but yields meaningful outcome! Overhaul your treasure chest of passwords, apps, websites, and alarms to welcome excellence.

Defend the Unitask

The way technology has developed over the last couple of decades has been a blessing in so many ways. We are no longer chained to our desks or land-line telephones. We can get so many things done at once from virtually anywhere—even while in transit. We can keep up-to-date on the latest news, whether it's international, national, or just on our personal social media feeds, without TV or radio. But is it a real blessing?

Just as the brain can only house one conscious thought at a time, according to Sandra Mann, "Multitasking is a myth. The brain can only focus on one task at a time. The most current research indicates a significant diminution in productivity—as much as 40 percent when we are multitasking." There is plenty of research to back this up, and there has been a profusion of articles on the topic in recent years. While the many upsides of being connected 24/7 are well documented, so are the many ways it is hurting us. It's widely reported that we are losing the ability to focus, connect meaningfully with others, and even be efficient! This is not a development I like.

The idea that we can e-mail, listen to music, exercise, and have a conversation with our friend simultaneously is a myth. If we are trying to do all of these things at the same time, what are the chances that we're doing any of them well? Can you relate to this issue? How do you try to multitask in your life? Do you find yourself forgetting things that may have appeared in your e-mail or that you might have heard in a conversation—things that would have found a more permanent space in your brain had you really focused? Do you sometimes set out to do one thing but then get sidetracked by something else, completely forgetting your initial intention?

I can't tell you how often these sorts of things happen to me. Annoying! My clients are often similarly overwhelmed. We all have a tendency to scatter our attention amongst the various needs and desires pulling us in different directions. The trick to multitasking is not to try to do everything at once, which is literally impossible, but to approach a set of tasks in succession, one after the other. Clear enough, right? While my clients like the sound of this in theory, they have a hard time executing on it because they have gotten so used to the concept of multitasking. Accomplishing a series of tasks in quick but isolated succession takes quite a bit of restraint. It takes practice. But there's a simple trick to it.

The unitask. Tackle your to-do list the way your brain is designed to: by concentrating on one task at a time. In an age of electronic multitasking and multiple distractions, defend the unitask! If you find yourself overwhelmed with everything you have to do in a short period of time, this Sweet Spot Check will help you.

 SWEET SPOT CHECK **DEFEND THE UNITASK**

- **Focus on the task at hand. List everything you have to do today by order of priority. Then focus on the most pressing task.**
- **Minimize distractions. While working, resist the urge to check e-mail or be available on IM. Set your phone aside. Disconnect from the Internet (or look into implementing software that blocks access to your e-mail) and silence your phone if necessary. Clear physical space (e.g., on your desk) and mental space (e.g., from potential social distractions) to set the stage for that top priority.**
- **Set a timer at intervals. If you will need to take breaks from that one task to attend to other things, you can set a timer (say, for every forty-five minutes) to signal when you may do so. Plus, it's a great idea to stand and stretch at forty-five-minute intervals, even do some deep breathing, to refresh yourself for further productivity. You can even read and respond to e-mails in batches at preset intervals, rather than making yourself constantly available and disrupting your work flow. If you must**

     break before the interval is up, make a conscious effort to break at a logical point in your work, rather than at random points.

- Group together smaller tasks: Cluster multiple admin calls (making doctor's appointments, following up on bills, etc.) or other niggling tasks that must get done into a single forty-five-minute stretch. It might require some focus and stamina to tackle them in succession, but it's a great way to get the job done and free up longer, uninterrupted stretches of time to focus on bigger tasks.
- When you've completed that first task, move on to the next top priority on your list, and then the next, clearing physical and mental space for each.

After falling into a rhythm with this unitasking challenge, clients have come back to me reporting increased productivity and diminished stress. They're surprised at how much more they can get done, and how much more present they can be. Excellence! Stop trying to multitask and forgetting things. Defend the unitask.

Compare Yourself (Really!)

I frequently hear my clients and friends compare themselves to others and get discouraged, undermining their self-worth. Whether they compare themselves to neighbors, friends, colleagues, even celebrities, or folks they only know via social media, the comparisons get them down. These comparisons stymie progress, sometimes deterring action completely: *What's the point of applying for the position when there are others who are so much more qualified than I am?* or *Why try to get healthy when I'll never be skinny and beautiful like that?* or *Everyone always seems to have somewhere cool to go. Why am I always home in my pajamas?*

In a workshop I conducted, all of the participants—who, on appearance, seemed happy, successful, and confident—agreed that it was *impossible* not to compare themselves to others. Tasha said she often felt stupid compared to others. Samantha felt others were more engaging, so she never tried to contribute meaningfully to conversations. Mark was puzzled about how easily networking came to others. Julie, who thought everyone else was better dressed, felt self-conscious about the way people looked at her when she walked into a room. Elliot felt as if he never fit in. Maddie felt insecure as a stay-at-home mom among a bunch of high-achieving professionals.

Compare and despair? It doesn't have to be that way! Some coaches will tell you to stop comparing, but I believe it's part of our wiring to compare things—people, objects, situations, what have you. Comparisons are ingrained in us. We use them to make sense of our world. They're inevitable. But we can stop using comparisons to beat ourselves down. If comparisons are an entrenched part of our emotional landscape, doesn't it make more sense to work *with* our comparisons rather than try unsuccessfully to fight them? Here are five ways to stop feeling defeated and use comparisons to your benefit.

SWEET SPOT CHECK **COMPARE YOURSELF**

- Compare and be inspired: Use other people's achieve-ments and accolades as motivation to create and act on your own goals instead of allowing them to crush your spirit. We all need role models whom we can emulate.
- Compare and learn: Figure out what's worked for others and see how you might incorporate some of their good ideas into your own strategy. Which of their habits or insights might benefit you?
- Compare and reroute: Remember, just because someone else is successful now doesn't mean they haven't made mistakes along the way. Learn from others' experiences to avoid pitfalls and delays. How can you learn from their experiences, even their failures?
- Compare and create: What new ideas can you come up with, based on concepts and strategies that you collect from others? How can they supplement or ignite your own good ideas?
- Compare and be grateful: You may not be as cool or as successful as the next person in your own mind (in their minds, you might just be, as they compare themselves to you!) but what is good about now—about who you are, who they are—today? Appreciate the differences and your own unique assets.

Don't stop comparing—just change the way you do it. Make the process productive! Noticing and finding inspiration in the experiences of others keeps you right in your sweet spot.

Peak Your Posture

Improving your posture is a really easy tactic for building and exuding confidence. Consciously or not, we all respond well to good posture, in ourselves and in others. When we carry ourselves upright, we inspire confidence, trust, and respect. We make excellent first impressions and project strength to the world.

Research shows that when we are sharing our feelings or opinions, our body language accounts for about 55 percent of what we communicate to the world. That's more than half of our message! Albert Mehrabian, a researcher on body language at UCLA, found that in these situations, words account for only 7 percent of our oral communications, with the balance—a whopping 93 percent—being body language, tone, inflection, and other sounds we make.

Another researcher, anthropologist Ray Birdwhistell, in his study of nonverbal communication, found that 65 percent of communication is done without the use of words. People form 60 to 80 percent of their initial opinion about a new person in less than four minutes (*The Definitive Book of Body Language*, pp. 9–10). Gosh, think about all of those reports, speeches, or breakup conversations you rehearsed over your lifetime. What did you focus on most when you prepped? Words! But it turns out that, unless you're writing a book or sending a written message, words are the least impactful part of your communications.

In fact, your body language plays the biggest role in conveying to the world what you feel about yourself, about the work that you're doing, and about the environment you're in. Before you even open your mouth, others already have a sense of what's going on in your head and have formed opinions of you. I always tell my clients that your brain has to do much less work if your body sends the right message first.

Unfortunately, many of us are unaware of the one thing that most obviously betrays a lack of confidence—poor posture. Have you ever noticed someone slumping over, crossing his arms, or fidgeting? What did those postures signal to you? Have you ever done the same? These common postures make it clear to others that you're not 100 percent comfortable in a situation, whether it's at work or in a social setting.

The good news is that improving your posture is an incredibly easy fix that doesn't require much brainpower. When I begin a coaching engagement with any client, one of the things we focus on first is his or her posture. It's low-hanging fruit because it doesn't require major shifts in attitudes or beliefs.

Sweet Spot Tip: Make eye contact. In a conversation, meet the other person's eyes. If you are in a group setting, look up from the floor so that your eyes are at others' eye level; then, when speaking, make an effort to engage with as many people as is reasonable simply by resting your eyes on theirs. When you do this, two benefits arise: your posture automatically improves and you engage with people with integrity.

Malia was widely considered a world-class expert in a high-profile consumer products business. Once people got to know her and her abilities, they were sold and had every faith that she was in fact essential to the company's success. I'll repeat that: *once people got to know her.* The problem? Malia made an uninspiring first impression. Malia would shuffle around the office hunched over, often with her arms crossed protectively across her chest. A common initial impression? Malia had no place in senior management. She did not inspire confidence in the least. Why was this unimpressive woman sitting in the corner office wielding all that power? She also failed to connect with the company's partners, which was important for the company's growth. What value could she possibly bring?

Malia needed to peak her posture to convey the message that she belonged and had things under control. Yes, all of this was possible to relay just through her posture. But she had been conveying the opposite and doing herself a great disservice.

Within just a few weeks of our engagement, Malia's CEO told me how delighted he was with her progress—how surprised he was at how quickly she'd effected meaningful change: She seemed "more comfortable in her skin, more self-assured, and better with people," he reported. What struck me as slightly amusing was that we hadn't even gotten to the heart of the transformation that Malia would experience in the following six months. Malia had merely peaked her posture. Standing tall, she now conveyed the message appropriate for her über-executive stature in her company.

Sweet Spot Tip: My clients find it illuminating to see themselves on video. We record them, and then we review the video to see what works and what doesn't. Even with just an eight-minute clip, my clients are often stunned to see what they're doing with their bodies and how distracting many of their physical mannerisms can be. When preparing for an interview or a big presentation, record yourself using the video camera on your computer or your PDA, and then watch for body language that detracts from the impactful message you want to deliver. I do this myself, especially when rehearsing speeches, so that I can monitor my tone, the speed at which I talk, and any odd habits that might distract my listeners from my intended message.

Stand up tall! I tell my clients that if they optimize that 55 percent (or even up to 80 percent) of what they communicate to the world with their physical presence, the rest of their work becomes much easier. That's more than half the effort without saying one word! Now it's your turn to use your body to convey maximum confidence. Get on your feet and try this next Sweet Spot Check.

SWEET SPOT CHECK **PEAK YOUR POSTURE**

- Plant both feet firmly on the ground. Think of your lower body as the strong foundation that supports the message you want to send out.
- Engage your belly. Pull it in! Doing this supports your diaphragm, which will allow you to speak with strength. Think of this as a natural extension of that strong foundation that begins at your feet.
- Puff your chest out (without flaring your ribs). This will straighten your spine and draw your shoulders back naturally. Relax your shoulders back and down. Let your arms rest at your sides from there. This posture maintains an openness to others, instead of shutting them out (e.g., by crossing your arms or slouching over). It also encourages deep breaths.
- Elongate the front of your neck. This helps to keep your eyes up and alert, facilitating eye contact and clear communication.
- Take up space. Make your presence apparent. Whether you have a big or small physique, shrinking back into a corner will *not* help you to project the confidence you want others to feel. Convey that you belong here as much as anyone else.

At first this may sound like a lot to remember, but with practice, this posture will come naturally and increase both your apparent and your genuine confidence. Your outward physicality absolutely affects the way you feel: If you stand confidently, you'll feel more confident inside, and others will take note. If you find the above steps confusing, just imagine a hefty cord hooked into the crown of your head, pulling your whole body upward, and your posture will fall into place.

This Peak Your Posture Sweet Spot Check also works when seated, which is important, especially in meetings. Practice sitting with good posture even when you're alone, whether at your desk or at the kitchen table (it's better for your back, your breathing, and your productivity, anyway), so that it comes naturally when you find yourself with others. During a meeting or a dinner, run down the mental checklist above to ensure that you remain engaged and engaging. Whoever you are with—colleagues, friends, family—will get the message that (a) you want to be there, and (b) you are comfortable and feel good about yourself in that situation.

Several years ago, when I conducted research on effective interviewing skills, I spoke with a lawyer, Rob, who said that posture was his number one strategy in interviewing for his first job. When Rob graduated from law school in the 1980s, it was a tough market. Solid jobs in New York City were scarce, and even the best of the graduating classes struggled for decent placements. There was certainly no dearth of high-performing law students from top law schools across the country who were willing to fill in those few coveted positions. Many of them failed in their attempts to land a first-year position.

Luckily for Rob, his sister had advised him on posture. Yes, Rob had earned high marks at his top-tier law school, and he had built a stellar résumé. But he knew, given the market, that even these accomplishments wouldn't cut it. There were so many others who fit that same profile. So he walked into these formidable law firms where the competition was fierce, he stood tall, and he sat before his interviewers in a way that told them he was totally engaged.

Rob applied to thirteen law firms and received twelve offers. Not one other person he knew achieved returns like that. His sister had been right. Rob chalked it up to his posture, which set him apart from the rest. As a senior partner now, Rob takes note of applicants' postures when he interviews them. He knows that their outward presence reflects what's happening inside. He also feels more of a connection with those who carry themselves with confidence, and is thus more inclined to move them on to the next round, if not give them an offer.

Sweet Spot Tip: When sitting for an interview, sit in the front half of your chair and lean slightly forward to exude an engaged, excellent energy. Resist the urge to laze back into your seat as it creates a physical gulf between you and your interviewer. As you lean forward to bridge the gap, you'll create a more excellent connection between you.

Sometimes, however, a person's body language can fool you. When I first started my coaching work, I ran a workshop for a group of fifteen high-school girls. They all sat around a conference room table, with me at the head. Directly across from me, at the other end of the long table, sat a girl, Eloise, who could not have looked less interested to be there. She seemed clearly annoyed! To be honest, it being one of my first workshops, this fifteen-year-old student intimidated the bejesus out of me with her very apparent disinterest. I was disappointed in myself for not being able to connect with her over the course of the five-hour workshop.

As it happened, that night, I received an e-mail message in bright fuchsia and italic font. From Eloise. It began, "Dear Karen, I can't thank you enough for making me feel important and showing me how I can work to reach my potential . . ." and then went on at length about how my work had really inspired her to work harder and aspire to more, despite the many obstacles in her life. I was stunned. I had totally misread Eloise's body language, which I now realized reflected her own discomfort with herself rather than her disinterest in me. Now, years later, when we meet for the occasional meal or just keep up with each other online, I marvel at Eloise's determination, excellent attitude, and accomplishments.

Sometimes, you'll have to look beyond someone else's body language to determine how he or she is truly feeling. By the same token, you'll want to be careful that your body language is sending the message you want others to hear loud and clear. So whether you're sitting, standing, or walking, remember to peak your posture. It's one of the simplest things you can do to bring yourself closer to your sweet spot.

Declutter Your Space

Over the last couple of years, there have been many times when my apartment was an unmitigated disaster. During a series of renovation and redecoration projects, dust and disorganization—total discombobulation at times—pervaded spaces that I'd usually kept clean and organized to the hilt.

During my office renovation, my work infiltrated my apartment— the dining room table, the living room ottoman, the kitchen counter, and sometimes even the kids' rooms. The entire contents of my old closets and shelves sat in plain view throughout the main living space. Even worse, when I needed to locate something, it took way more time than it should have. This is a real problem for someone who likes a neat and orderly environment, and to run an efficient operation.

Truth: My surroundings drove me entirely insane. Since I work out of my home office, there was no escape. I was short with my family, and my annoyance grew daily. I just wanted a sense of order, for criminy's sake! When it got to be too much, I'd initiate a major decluttering project, exercising zero tolerance for belongings that could be passed on or thrown out. Phew.

Reflecting on those periods of unrest makes me think about how an organized, uncluttered work space is essential for clarity, calmness, and productivity. Instead of wasting time looking for things and wasting energy being annoyed, set aside time to create a space that is conducive to your ability to think, feel, and breathe. Such a space is essential to your sweet spot.

Recently, well after my office renovation was completed, it was just papers that got to me. Piles of bills. Stacks of kids' school projects. Client notes. Mailings. Sure, tucked away in discreet spots, but unattended nonetheless. To boot, it was the end of a season, when I like to spend a few hours culling out my closet, to send clothing and shoes to my family and their churches in the Philippines.

I spent six or seven gratifying hours between a Friday evening and early Saturday morning organizing my work space, with music jamming in the background. I filed important papers where they needed to be, threw out garbage, and took care of business I'd overlooked for too long. Then I moved on to my closet: I pulled out blouses, dresses, and shoes that I'd grown tired of, but which were in great shape to be donated or passed on to women in need. At the end of that Saturday morning, I could breathe again! My desk, instead of driving me away, welcomed me with its cleanliness. I felt a distinct lightness that had eluded me for months.

Now, you might not enjoy organizing your physical space as much as I do, and you might even have a higher tolerance for clutter than I do, but the benefits of decluttering are universal. Take a look around you right now, whether you're at home or in your work space. I imagine, if you're like most human beings, you have some things in disarray that you overlook because they've sat there for so long. Or there may be a clutter zone that triggers a negative thought every time you walk by it (*I'm such a mess!* or *Why can't I get it together?*)

On the other end of the spectrum, imagine your space as a place that inspires you, that gets your creative juices flowing. Imagine that, every time you walk into your space, you feel a sense of clarity and calm. Here, you can refresh your mind and really think, breathe, and get things done. No, this is not some fantasy—it is entirely within your grasp!

What does your work or living space look like? Does it make you feel good, clean, and light? Or does it fuel negative thoughts? If the

Sweet Spot Tip: Declutter room by room, or spot by spot. Taking on your entire home or office at once may just discourage you entirely and keep you in the same clutter. So commit to one trouble spot and finish it before moving on to the next one. Unitask!

latter, give it a total makeover. By clearing away the physical clutter, you'll clear away the clutter in your head and your heart, too.

SWEET SPOT CHECK **DECLUTTER YOUR SPACE**

- Determine which space you want to declutter—whether it's a work space or a living space. Consider the size of the project and set aside enough time to get the job done. (I find a Friday night very effective because forgoing a night out compels me to maximize productivity, and there's no work the next day.)
- Prepare by purchasing any storage helpers—bins, cabinets, stacking shelves, etc.—that will help you organize your space more effectively. (Personally, I *love* the Container Store. I could spend hours wandering its aisles, marveling at the simple ingenuity of their wares.)
- Put on some fun music that will keep you motivated but focused. Resist the TV and the telephone so you don't get sidetracked.
- Start with one area of clutter—and attack. Be absolutely merciless! Find a place for every single thing that's been sitting there, whether it belongs in a file cabinet, a Salvation Army bag, or the garbage.
- Move on to the next area of clutter and repeat, and then again and again, until the whole space looks and feels like new.
- Add a scented candle, a framed picture, or an inviting bouquet of flowers for that extra touch. Take a deep breath and enjoy your new space.
- Schedule a monthly or bimonthly decluttering session to maintain the order you've achieved, since clutter has an uncanny way of creeping back when you're not paying attention.

Sometimes it takes reaching the end of your rope to get motivated to declutter. Once you hit that wall, use your frustration to spur you to action. Imagine the lightness and freedom of working and living in a clean, clutter-free environment. Think of all the mental and emotional energy that you can now devote to your sweet spot.

Experiment

I will never forget the first time I undertook a juice cleanse. I recall the apprehension, the disdain, and the total disgust—in that order. It was not a pretty sight.

Years ago, before juice cleanses came into vogue, my dear friend Alexis suggested I try one that she loved. "Don't worry," she said, "you won't miss eating. The woman who does this cleanse is a chef, so her juices are absolutely delicious!" At the time, I was always game for the next cool diet, and, feeling a bit puffy, I was ready for something new.

Day one: six juices. The first juice of the day was a tiny cup of wheatgrass—very strong, but not bad. I could shoot it back much as I had shot back many kamikazes in my college years. Easy. The second of the day was a tall green vegetable juice. At sixteen ounces, it was another story entirely. I swear, I could taste the dirt that the greens had sprouted from—repulsive! But somehow, I managed to choke it down and get through the rest of that first day.

The second and third days of the cleanse were not so pretty. Alexis's words echoed in my head: "You won't miss eating." Really, Lex? Really? For someone who delighted in Spam, processed foods, and lots of chocolate, slugging down a sixteen-ounce container of liquefied greens was a tremendous feat. Nonetheless, I pushed through, hovering over the sink to catch whatever came dribbling out the sides of my mouth.

Day four. The final straw. I immediately called Alexis: "I just threw up!" Her response? "Oh my God! Are you pregnant?" Am I pregnant? *Am I pregnant?* No! In my head, I was screaming, *I can't believe I listened to you and agreed to do this stupid cleanse!!*

But with her encouragement, I persevered, and by the end of that same day, I felt and looked totally different. My eyes were whiter, I had amazing energy, and I felt wonderfully revitalized. Even more surprising, I continued juicing after the cleanse. Now that I realized how much better I could feel, I actually learned to enjoy green juices and healthier fare on a daily basis.

This experience opened up my mind and my taste buds to an entirely different way of looking at food. Instead of thinking of food as merely a way to satiate hunger or indulge a craving, I could now appreciate it as a precious source of energy and vitality. This was a huge discovery—one that might have eluded me to this day, if I hadn't tried the cleanse. As irritated as I was with Alexis initially, I will forever be grateful to her for introducing me to a new experience.

Many of my clients have experimented with different behaviors at work. One client in particular, Cole, played a big role in his company's corporate structure. He was an incredibly intelligent guy who achieved major wins for his organization. Cole, however, was not totally comfortable in his leadership role, and it didn't come naturally to him to connect with others. In order to continue to lead the company on an upward trajectory, he knew he had to experiment with different strategies, even those he was uncomfortable with.

In an effort to facilitate bonding and generate loyalty, Cole implemented a combination of the following activities for himself and his team:

- more frequent staff social events
- one-on-one lunches with key staff members
- regular communication with the entire company via all-hands meetings and company-wide e-mail updates

Such activities may sound easy enough to you, but they put Cole way outside his comfort zone. He was no fan of small talk or socializing. Still, Cole resolved to experiment with the above action items, and after some initial discomfort, he started to find it easier to connect with his team. And as a result, they felt more inspired and delivered a better work product.

My belief in experimentation can be traced back to my high school, Punahou School (President Barack Obama's alma mater as well). Looking back on those years, I am not surprised that many of my old schoolmates have pursued incredibly interesting, nontraditional careers. In addition to the doctors, lawyers, dentists, teachers, and bankers amongst us, I also know:

- entrepreneurs
- glassblowers
- jewelry makers
- video game designers
- filmmakers
- symphony conductors
- technology trailblazers
- negotiators
- fashion designers
- fitness instructors
- endurance athletes

I could go on. I believe this fabulous array of careers came to fruition because Punahou encouraged us to explore our interests through nontraditional classes and career exposure. Several of my schoolmates first discovered their sweet spots at Punahou, and went on to pursue careers accordingly. Others, like myself, took a more circuitous route but carried the gift of experimentation into adulthood.

Think about your own experiences. What have you always wanted to try? What scares you that might provide a jolt of personal discovery? How can you stretch the boundaries of your comfort zone to find your sweet spot? You can't appreciate what you've never tried. This applies to anything in life, great or small—whether it's trying a new cuisine, exploring a different city, building a relationship, starting a new job, enrolling in a cooking class, experimenting with an exercise regimen, or striking up a conversation with a stranger. The possibilities are endless. So stop saying "no," or even "maybe," to a new adventure. Get out there and experiment!

SWEET SPOT CHECK   **EXPERIMENT**

- **Pick an area of your life where you'd like to make a change, where you'd like to see improvement. Perhaps you want to be better at your job, become less inhibited around others, spice up a relationship, or explore a new career.**
- **Identify an activity that you can experiment with to effect desired change in this area of your life. It could be as simple as trying a new restaurant or singing karaoke, or as ambitious as learning a new language, traveling to an alien country, or volunteering for a cause that is meaningful to you.**
- **Commit to this activity and see it through. Explore it long enough to get past any initial discomfort and let the experience sink in. Notice how it makes you feel as you explore it further. Do you notice a shift in mindset? (*Hey, I can do this!*) What new ideas or experiences does this ignite for you?**

You can experiment with almost anything. It doesn't have to be super ambitious or foreign. Starting small often paves the way for more adventure and bigger perceptual shifts. If you don't want to go it alone, invite a like-minded friend to join you. Just remember that it is totally normal to experience some discomfort during your new adventure. It's part of the process. Read on.

Embrace Discomfort

Working through the discomfort of a new experience can yield excellent growth and satisfaction. Whether you are experimenting with a new nutrition plan, going on a blind date, taking on a new project at work, or adjusting to the challenges of being a new parent, by embracing discomfort, you can find your hidden sweet spot.

Even smaller changes come with a discomfort zone. Imagine something as simple as deciding to wake up forty-five minutes earlier in the morning to fit in a meditation. Your body must adjust. Discomfort. Or you resolve to speak up during a meeting instead of letting others push their agendas ahead of yours. Your mind must adjust. Discomfort. Bigger changes, of course, bring greater discomfort.

At the gym one day, I overheard a trainer encouraging his client on the elliptical machine. (I don't know her, but let's call her Amanda.) Only moments after she began her first interval, I heard her exclaim in almost hysterical panic: "I can't! I can't! *I can't!!*" But Amanda's trainer calmly and firmly supported her: "Yes, yes, you can. You can do this."

With much protestation and despite a hefty belief and genuine fear that she couldn't, Amanda finished her intervals. To be honest, I was surprised that she'd greeted such a seemingly small feat with such panic and doubt. For me, this form of exercise was totally in my comfort zone. While I empathized that this might be scary for her, there was another part of me that thought, *Just get it done, lady. It's not that big a deal.* And ultimately, she did. At the end, the smile on her face made it clear that she'd surprised herself.

Later that same day, during my voice lesson, I started singing—only to be stopped within seconds. "You're not giving enough," my teacher, Sharon, said. "Karen, I know you can give me more." I wasn't sure what she was asking. As she repeatedly stopped me and asked for more, my frustration set in, as did an acute desire to give up. Then, *I* started to panic. *I'm not cut out for this! What am I doing here?* Sound familiar? Discomfort.

At that moment, I was no different from Amanda. Our discomfort zones were just different. I was nervous that I wouldn't be able to deliver the depth that my voice teacher was looking for. She'd asked me to sing with emotion, feeling, and volume—a style of singing that wasn't remotely in my wheelhouse. I found it enormously difficult and wanted to retreat. But when I persevered, the sounds that came out of my mouth surprised me. Despite my initial doubt, I sang the melody in tune, with confidence, emotion, and musicality. It was invigorating!

By stepping into and working through our respective discomfort zones—experiences of real fear and doubt—Amanda and I summoned a whole new level of energy and effort. What we found on the other side was exhilaration, a new sense of achievement that we had not thought possible.

Sweet Spot Tip: If you can't hire a professional, be your own coach or trainer. Talk yourself through and to the other side of that discomfort. Imagine that you are encouraging a friend to do something that scares her. What would you say to her? Turn it around and use those same words on yourself.

Matthew has worked his way up the ranks at a philanthropic organization and, for years, has preferred to fly under the radar. When he first came to me, Matthew told me that no matter what he did, and no matter what value he knew he contributed, he always felt like an imposter when it came to meeting with strangers. Matthew felt that people always looked right through him, thinking that he was extraneous. The problem was that part of his job was to connect with donors and play host in social situations.

Another client, Victoria, ran a large consumer-facing company. As with any top executive, her job entailed representing the company, requiring her to step up to the podium to make speeches and strategic connections with key management at other companies to create new alliances. The trouble for Victoria was, despite her achievements, she felt like a loser whom no one wanted to talk to. The result: She held herself back from meeting potential business partners.

With both Matthew and Victoria, we began by cultivating self-love and creating mantras to gird themselves in uncomfortable situations. Then they started to practice putting themselves out there in social situations. Little by little and bit by bit, they worked through their discomfort zones and taught themselves that, in fact, they could be comfortable in these environments.

What's your discomfort zone? The following Sweet Spot Check will help you work throughout it.

 SWEET SPOT CHECK **EMBRACE DISCOMFORT**

- Identify an activity, environment, or situation with which you'd like to become more comfortable. What in your life do you find particularly challenging or scary that meets with internal resistance and halts desired progress?
- Examine that challenging situation closely. Dig deep. What about it sparks fear or panic in you? Is your reaction informed by certain negative experiences in the past that have become negative beliefs? Does it have to do with a lack of self-love or confidence?
- Based on your answers, adopt any of the Sweet Spot Checks that will help you push through your discomfort zone—such as Cultivate Self-Love, Know Your Worth, Sweeten Your Beliefs, and Choose Your Mantra.
- Embrace the discomfort. As it arises, instead of running away, move toward it. Recognize it as a necessary

agent of growth. Remember, the greater the change, the greater the discomfort.

- If necessary, hire a coach, trainer, teacher, or other professional to help you work through this particular challenge. If hiring someone is not an option, enlist the support of a friend to hold you accountable. If you'd rather work through it on your own, talk yourself through the panic or resistance. Be positive but firm, and keep reminding yourself to breathe.

- Take note of how you feel as you embrace your discomfort and accept the challenge. Repeat this exercise again and again, until you no longer resist or want to run away. Then celebrate your newfound courage!

No matter what level of discomfort you experience as you effect desired change, remember that it is a temporary feeling, and one that will lead you to excellence on the other side.

Make a Bucket List

Years ago, to provide a solid, informed foundation for my workshops and coaching practice, I interviewed roughly two hundred successful women and men from all over the world. One of the many questions I asked was what their greatest regrets, if any, had been during their life journeys. The leading regret that these individuals reported was not enough globetrotting. Whether they had never gone abroad or had traveled to more than fifty countries, their wanderlust seemed limitless.

Travel abroad has impacted my life immensely. I met Jay in Hong Kong. I lived, worked, and gave birth to my first child in London, and I traveled from there to South America, Africa, and all over Europe. Travel has profoundly enriched my life, professionally and personally. It is a humbling experience to get a firsthand glimpse of what the world has to offer, and to realize that we only have a lifetime to explore it.

If, as for most people, travel ranks high on your wish list, you need to plan for it. Without a plan, another year will come and go, and that place you've always dreamed of seeing will remain just that—a dream. That's why we need our bucket lists, you know one of those lists of all the things that you want to do in your life before you kick the proverbial bucket.

My friend Sam and her husband Jesse live in New York City. Since they have access to their family's lovely beach home, an easy three-hour flight away, for a long time they simply went on the same vacation there every year. When I introduced the idea of a bucket list, they immediately took action and came up with a list of new places they wanted to see and started booking different adventures. Over the last year, instead of defaulting to their family's beach home, they've vacationed in Los Angeles, Mexico, and Hawaii and are beyond thrilled that they have! They have also planned trips to Africa and other distant destinations.

What does travel have to do with your sweet spot? First, it's about seizing the day and minimizing regret. Certainly, life is too short *not* to live in your sweet spot. Travel opens your eyes wide to all the beauty and opportunity around you, and fills your heart with gratitude.

Second, travel breeds inspiration. Seeing how people in other cultures live, work, struggle, and succeed—whether abroad or within our borders—broadens your perspective and sparks new ideas. For example, it might spark a business idea, or inspire you to approach relationships differently. You'll discover new customs, cuisines, and rituals—some of which may stay with you for the rest of your life. You may learn new routes to your sweet spot.

Sweet Spot Tip: Have you ever traveled solo? Traveling on your own gives you the freedom to see and do what you want, in your own time. You have the luxury of reconnecting with yourself. Traveling alone also makes you more open to engaging with natives and fellow travelers. I know it can be scary (embrace discomfort!), but solitude and new experiences are a good combination for testing and surpassing limits.

Third, if you are traveling with friends, a significant other, or family, you create new bonds and memories that you can't create in your everyday routines. Last year, my family traveled to Beijing, China, and Siem Reap, Cambodia. On this trip, my kids took a break from bickering, discovered games and conversations they both enjoyed, and now seek each other's companionship in ways they hadn't before. My husband and I also take regular trips by ourselves, leaving the kids at home so we can reconnect as a couple. Even when I travel solo, I welcome the chance to reconnect with myself.

Here's your Sweet Spot Check to make your dream destinations a reality.

SWEET SPOT CHECK **MAKE A BUCKET LIST**

- List all the places you'd like to see in your lifetime, in order of priority. Include destinations near and far—whatever calls out to your personal wanderlust.
- Examine your calendar for the next year or two and identify windows of time that would allow for travel to your top one or two destinations.
- Figure out your budget. Can you afford to travel to your top destination this year? What deals might you find to make it affordable? If it's too much to swing this year, perhaps plan to travel there next year and start saving up for it now. In the meantime, you can set your sights on a more feasible trip.
- Book the trip. Start with flights and then hotels. If you're a do-it-yourself type, there are countless travel publications and online resources to help you book the trip you want, no matter what your budget. However, I recommend finding a great travel agent whom you can trust to get you good deals and ensure that you love where you end up. This can be a big time saver.
- Look forward to your upcoming travels! Much of the fun of booking a trip is the anticipation of discovering a new place. Pick the restaurants and the special sites you'd like to visit. Think about what you might like to explore and experience. Book anything in advance that requires it, leaving some time free for pure relaxation and spontaneity.
- Enjoy and be in the moment! The logistics of getting to and from your destination can be stressful, but remember, it's all a part of the adventure. Keep an open mind (things in life don't always go exactly as planned) and savor the novelty of the experience. This is the moment you've been waiting for—so breathe it in and be awash in gratitude!
- Repeat all of the above, again and again.

If money is an issue, start a travel fund and put money aside every month. One woman I interviewed took on extra work so that she could maintain such a fund—she wanted it that badly. Or opt for excursions that are more local and less costly. Whatever your situation is, refuse to set the stage for future regret and get cracking on your bucket list!

And if it just so happens that travel is not so high on your wish list, keep in mind that a bucket list can encompass *anything* and *everything* you fantasize about doing in your life. Commit these happy thoughts to writing and maximize your chances of experiencing them in your lifetime!

Express Yourself

I've talked a fair amount about the language we use when we talk to ourselves. I'd like to take this theme a step further to give expression to those deeper thoughts and feelings that make us feel vulnerable and that we therefore sometimes prefer to ignore.

We live in a world where technology dumbs down emotion. We exchange countless e-mails, IMs, and text messages each day, and yet we cannot always accurately discern the feelings behind the words, which on many occasions gives rise to confusion. Also, when dealing with situations that threaten to unmask our genuine feelings, it's all too easy to default to the anonymity and safety of technology. For example, we might send texts to express anger, sadness, or deep affection. The irony is that these are usually the times when authentic, thoughtful communication and honest self-expression can strengthen connections.

Actually expressing what we feel—everything from deep sadness to total elation—helps us to live and thrive in our sweet spots. I like to think of the range of our emotions as a bandwidth. The more we allow ourselves to experience and express, the more elastic the band, and the more expansive the range of our feelings. The full breadth of our emotions is an innate gift that too many of us suppress. The less we allow ourselves to feel, the less we give life to our feelings and the shallower and more muted they become. Conversely, as we get comfortable with expressing the full range of our emotions, we become better at releasing anger and experiencing greater bliss. The relief is palpable.

While it is important to sweeten our beliefs, detox our vocabulary, choose supportive mantras, and celebrate our wins—all in order to tap into the power of a productive mindset—it is also important to give constructive space to negative feelings. It may not be easy, but it is a vital part of the sweet spot strategy. Those negative feelings are there, and they need attention. Ignoring them won't make them go away. Suppressed emotions persist, coming out when we least expect them to, often manifesting in unpleasant ways (think acne, disordered eating, disease, stress, fatigue, or unwelcome emotional outbursts).

For years, I did not cry. I laughed, I smiled, and I felt happy enough. But I never cried. When I was angry, it would take a lot of coaxing and cajoling to get me to admit why I was upset. Instead, I would stew and wait for the anger to subside. In my mind, negative feelings had no place in my happy life. They were scary, uncontrollable emotions that I thought were better left unexpressed. I was trying to protect my happy spot. The thing is, those unexpressed negative feelings remained alive inside me, whether I realized it or not.

At a seminar with Tony Robbins, I distinctly remember one exercise. Before we began, Tony warned us not to comfort those who were crying around us because experiencing the full sensation of sadness was integral to the process. My thought at the time? *I am going to be the only idiot here, out of 4,500 people, who can't shed a tear.*

Fortunately for my self-conscious self, I did. A lot. It felt amazing! And those tears were just the first of many to flow from then until now. You might not think that's a good development, but in fact, it is. Now, I can be vulnerable. I have learned how to share anger productively instead of holding onto it. I am more empathetic with the sadness and frustration in others because I am able to recognize and accept those feelings in myself.

Best of all, because I am comfortable giving full expression to my negative feelings, I can also step up to vulnerability on the other side. Now, I can express glee and elation, which I also had suppressed for

Sweet Spot Tip: There may be moments when your emotions far surpass your ability to express them in words. Sometimes, you just have to scream or break down in tears. When that happens, scream into a pillow. Find a safe place to cry your heart out. You'll diffuse the intensity of your emotion by releasing it, and then you'll be able to move on to the next step: constructive self-expression.

fear of seeming silly or exposing too much of my genuine self. Having stretched out my emotional bandwidth, I can feel even greater happiness and joy. I am so grateful for my tears because, thanks to them, I am now comfortable enough with the intensity of my feelings to allow myself to feel and express total bliss!

Relationships thrive on emotions, so learning how to express your feelings in a constructive way will strengthen your relationships. It's your choice. You can be honest and work through negative emotions as they arise, or else try to suppress them, feeding an internal groundswell that will eventually overwhelm you and affect the people around you.

But it's really the flexibility and the range of your entire emotional bandwidth that I want you to discover. It is only when you allow yourself to access your vulnerability that you can express your sadness and frustration and then, in turn, experience unadulterated joy. You smile more, you laugh louder, and your heart sings! You share your bliss more freely. It is truly an excellent state. If all of this sounds like alien territory to you, use this Sweet Spot Check to familiarize yourself with your own emotional landscape.

 SWEET SPOT CHECK **EXPRESS YOURSELF**

- Get in the habit of recognizing your emotions as they arise. Allow yourself to feel them without judgment. Which emotions come up frequently? Which seldom do? How intense or muted do they feel? If it helps, write your answers down in a journal and explore where you think these emotions come from.
- When you experience a feeling of sadness, shame, frustration, or anything that doesn't feel good, instead of suppressing it or looking for a distraction, embrace the discomfort. Experience the emotion, accept it for what it is, and then release it.

- If you are someone who has trouble expressing emotions to others, start with positive ones, even if they're just observations. Practice with simple but heartfelt statements, such as "I'm grateful to you," or "You've made my day," or "I love what you're wearing." Say such things out loud, and notice how it makes both of you feel.
- If your negative emotions involve someone else, ask yourself the following: (a) Does this person play a significant role in my life? and (b) Is this a recurring emotion that is unlikely to resolve itself if I don't express it? If your answer to both of these questions is yes, figure out a way to express your feelings to that person in a nonthreatening, productive way. Set aside a time to talk and listen to each other. Embrace vulnerability and express yourself with "I" statements, as in, "I am sad because . . . I was frustrated when . . ." instead of casting accusatory "You" statements, as in, "You made me feel . . . You always . . ." It may bring up some discomfort, but if you make that other person understand that you are expressing yourself in a spirit of trust and with a genuine desire to improve relations, he or she will respond in kind.
- As you stop judging and stifling your negative feelings and give expression to them, notice how much fuller your positive feelings are on the other end.

Find the words to express *all* of your feelings. You can talk them through with a close friend, a family member, or a professional listener such as a coach or a therapist. If you like to write, write about your emotions in a journal; this can have a tremendously cleansing effect. Whether you work through them on your own or with someone else, the most important thing is that you give space to your feelings and let them exist without judgment.

You can also use creative forms of expression. Clients I've worked with have found effective creative outlets via dance, yoga, and fictional writing. If there are emotionally charged stories bubbling inside of you, find a way to give them voice—verbally, musically, or otherwise. Constructive self-expression is a great healer.

Listen and Learn

As important as it is to express yourself, I will go out on a limb and say that it's even more important to listen. Word to the wise: There are teachers where you least expect them, and the act of listening enriches your life and deepens your connections with those around you.

No one knows everything, and certainly, we don't always know the most ideal paths for ourselves. Listening to others can elucidate your own journey to your sweet spot. Their lessons can become your lessons. It is stunning how much you learn when you take time to quiet your own voice, pause your mental chatter, and tune in to the wisdom of others. You are not an island. Not only can you find a world of support out there, but you can find shortcuts in your own evolution and excellence by learning from other people's experiences.

When I first started my workshops with high-school girls, I encountered one girl who, after almost every point I made, said, "Oh yeah, we did this at school," or "I learned this in my judo class," or "I know, we already practice this here." Every time she interjected, I persevered for the sake of the other girls, who listened attentively and volunteered new insights. While the rest of her classmates sent me e-mails telling me how much they'd learned from our time together and genuinely thanking me for my efforts, she remained silent. I was not surprised. She'd shut down her own capacity to learn because, in her mind, she already knew it all.

Sweet Spot Tip: Resist the urge to say, "Yeah, I've done that," even if you have, and "I know," even if you do. Instead, listen to someone else's perspective and insights on the same topic. You might learn something new.

Let go of the need to be the person who knows everything. In an extraordinarily inspiring TED Talk, Ric Elias, a businessman who survived the Hudson River airplane crash in January 2009, said: "I'm no longer trying to be right. I choose to be happy." Such a liberating insight!

Are you a receptive listener, or do you sometimes shut down learning opportunities without meaning to? Listen and learn with the following Sweet Spot Check.

 SWEET SPOT CHECK **LISTEN AND LEARN**

- Treat everyone around you as a potential teacher. Actively listen to your partners, friends, colleagues, family members, and even strangers. Take in their experiences and insights, and value their different perspectives.
- Observe your conversational habits. Are you both listening and sharing your ideas and feelings, or are you talking and then just waiting for your turn to talk again? Do you listen respectfully, or do you tend to interrupt or talk over others?
- Cease saying, "I know." It shuts down any opportunity to learn and indicates to the other person that you're not really listening. Instead, consider "Really?" or "Tell me more!"
- When someone suggests that something has "changed his or her life," listen attentively to their transformative experience (they will really appreciate it) and then consider what the same or a similar experience could do for you.
- Consider the people in your social media network. Are there people with whom you might especially enjoy having a face-to-face conversation? Reach out to them, explaining your interest in learning from them. Chances are, they will be flattered and receptive to your overture.

You may even be surprised with an instant and meaningful connection.

- Be open to a variety of learning opportunities. Spend time browsing in the self-help sections of your local bookstore. Sign up for self-development classes or seminars. You'd be surprised at the caliber and variety of resources available to you.
- Look for little bits of wisdom in your everyday conversations with your friends and family. Don't assume you already know everything about them. They, like you, are continually growing and evolving. Show interest and curiosity. Observe and listen.

Be open to others who can help you find your sweet spot. Whether it's in a formal setting (e.g., a conference, a workshop, a coaching session) or just a casual conversation with a friend, see what nuggets of truth you can glean and apply to your own life. Sometimes, for me, it's a single inspiring statement—"I'm no longer trying to be right. I choose to be happy." (You could while away hours on any given afternoon listening to those TED Talks, and it would be an incredibly productive use of your time.) Sometimes my kids are the best teachers. Take lessons and experience growth from unexpected places.

Part IV

Integrate Your Sweet Spot

"Still round the corner there may wait
A new road for you or a secret gate."

—J.R.R. Tolkien, *Lord of the Rings*

You're almost there! Part IV will help you to integrate all that you've learned about yourself in the previous pages and to really access your sweet spot. What follow are strategies that will help you wield your sweet spot at work, at play, and in love. You can call on these strategies whether you are looking within or outside of yourself.

See It Done

More often than not, when we think about working toward our goals, we think about the what-ifs, the obstacles we may encounter, and the possibility that we may fail. In considering all the impediments, we often lose sight of our star—the dream itself, which was initially so inspiring. Remember the perfectionist affliction of all or nothing? Because of this, we often talk ourselves out of achieving what we want before we even begin. Or else we become distracted and get rerouted down a different path.

Here's one tip that I share in my workshops that will help you to stay the course. Visualize exactly what it is you want. Or, *see it done*. This just means that instead of seeing all of the obstacles that prevent you from reaching your star, or letting the many distractions of daily life cloud your vision, actually envision what it would be like to achieve your goals. Imagine what it would look like, feel like, taste like, smell like. Put yourself smack-dab in the middle of your dream. Then look around, take in your surroundings, and savor what it's like to be there.

This differs from building out your star, where you consciously determine your goals and intellectually map out your routes and strategies. Seeing it done, you channel the full experience of manifesting your star. By invoking all your senses, all the powers of your imagination, and the full bandwidth of your emotions, you can see it so clearly, it's as if it has already happened!

In my workshops, I walk participants through a twelve-minute visualization in which they can see it done. During this guided meditation, they envision a day in their life twenty years from now. I walk them through every detail of waking up, how their bodies feel, their morning routine, who's around them, what they're wearing, where they are going, what they're doing when they get there, what activities they enjoy, what their meals are like, and so on—until the moment they fall asleep that night. Along the way, I ask them to summon smells, sights, colors, sounds, tastes, and other physical sensations. I ask them whom they're seeing, who and what makes them smile, and what they're grateful for. This form of imaginary time travel can yield such a vivid experience that they feel it in their bones.

The results of this visualization have surprised many of my workshop participants. They often see details, large and small, that they hadn't contemplated while building out their stars. Sometimes what they visualize during our meditation is quite different from what they'd originally conceived. (This is because mapping out your star and visualizing it through guided meditation exercises different parts of the brain; one is more intellectual, while the other is more emotional, even spiritual.) Other times, their visualizations adhere pretty closely to their original goals. Either way, seeing it done allows my clients to get really clear on what they want and where they want to go. It's an effective way to strengthen resolve and rev up motivation.

One participant, Todd, took this visualization very seriously. In twenty years, he still saw himself as a trainer (yes, he loves what he does, and he's really good at it), but he imagined himself living a bicoastal life, dividing his time between New York and Los Angeles. In his imagination, he owned two homes that he loved and was proud of. The clarity of his vision overwhelmed him. It was all so vivid and exhilarating!

Now keep in mind that Todd's a guy who doesn't have the luxury of a significant financial cushion. He doesn't make the kind of money that you associate with a glamorous bicoastal lifestyle. And yet, this was his vision. He was determined to make it happen from the second he walked out of that workshop.

Within weeks, Todd began a serious mission to find a house that would fit his bicoastal dream. Within months, he found one in New York, signed a contract, and closed. Shortly after that, Todd began to clean up and renovate the main house, where he would live, and the apartments within the house, which he intended to rent out to cover his mortgage.

I was so proud of Todd! Within a short period of time, he achieved his first major step toward his vision. He now owns a sweet house in a lovely community on Long Island, and has tenants whose rents cover his mortgage. He's already set his sights on a second home. Todd's bicoastal dream is that much closer to becoming a reality. Todd saw it done.

One of my friends, Sheila, had been surfing my website when she came upon a TV interview in which I'd described this exact visualization exercise. So she took it upon herself to do it on her own. Sheila found some reflection time, put on some music, and envisioned a day in her life ten years from now (yes, you can adjust the number of years according to what you want to accomplish). This, Sheila said, was particularly helpful because she'd come upon a fork in the road and wasn't clear on which direction to take.

Once she saw it done, though, her path became clearer. Instead of going through the intellectual process of weighing the pros and cons of what she wanted to pursue, Sheila let the images of her future career come to her. As a result of her visualization, she resumed her book project, got two articles picked up for publication, and explored various programs available for graduate studies in social work. She moved beyond the fork.

Now it's your turn. Close your eyes and envision your future. Let your subconscious dreams speak to you. The positive emotions and vivid sensory details that arise from this exercise will clarify your star and help to carry you over any obstacles.

SWEET SPOT CHECK   **SEE IT DONE**

- Set aside at least thirty minutes for quiet reflection in a private environment where you won't be distracted. You will need about twelve minutes for the visualization and another fifteen or more to write it all down.

- Go to www.findyoursweetspot.com to download the "See It Done" guided visualization. Get comfortably seated, close your eyes, and flash forward to a day in your life twenty years from now. Let my voice guide you through every detail of the day, from the moment you wake in the morning to the moment you drift off to sleep at night. Open your heart and mind to let your subconscious speak to you. Fully unleash your imagination to visualize your star.

- If you choose to do this visualization exercise on your own, without the audio download, play music that inspires you and expands your inner vision.

- Begin with a question. Ask yourself what you really desire, whether it's in a year, five years, or twenty years— you pick a timeframe that works for you. Be honest with yourself. Don't hold back. For example, if you want to own a new house, to live in a new city, or to end up in an entirely different career—or all three—then let that be what you picture. Think completely outside of your current box, if that's what you truly want, but hold onto what you already love about your life.

- Close your eyes, submit to the audio guide or the music, and let yourself experience a day in this ideal life you've created. Start with the moment you wake in the morning and picture every single moment that *ideally* follows— breakfast, exercise, getting dressed, going to work, seeing friends, sitting at your desk, etc. Don't miss a step!

- Be bold and creative. Let yourself go. Really open yourself emotionally to each part of your day, to every sensory detail. Allow yourself to feel all the love, passion, happiness, confidence, gratitude, and fulfillment that this life affords you.

- At the end of your visualization, write it all down. Record every feeling and sensation you experienced. Be as descriptive as possible. Recall colors, sounds, smells, tastes, textures. The more senses you can infuse into your writing, the more vivid it will be.

Having seen it done, reflect on how you feel. Consider whether you're already living your dream or whether you need to start making some significant changes. While maintaining this vision clearly in your mind, devise action steps that will get you to where you want to be. Act now! If any of the simpler elements of your visualization resonate as great ways to upgrade your life, incorporate them *immediately* into your daily routine. You don't need to wait out the twenty years to see them happen! For example, at one point in Sheila's vision, she dreamed of enjoying a hot breakfast in the morning. So she whipped up a delicious one for herself the very next day.

Reread your visualization regularly. If you feel compelled, take the time to revise the star that you devised earlier. Add to or subtract from it to incorporate the images you saw done to maintain the accuracy of your goals and dreams. Keep the experience fresh in your mind and close to your heart as you continue your journey to your star.

Sweet Spot Tip: Break your vision down into an action plan. Once you see it done, figure out what series of steps you must take to get there. Make a one-year plan, then a six-month plan, and then a monthly itinerary. If you need to start with a longer timeline than a year, map that out too. Breaking down your longer-term strategy into shorter-term plans will make your vision tangible.

Carve Out Me Time

You matter! Your time is precious. Unfortunately, many people—especially, but not exclusively, parents—put themselves at the tail end of their to-do lists. We take care of our children, address our spouse's needs, and worry about how much we're failing to do. We put ourselves dead last. It's not gender-specific: I find in my practice that men and women both struggle with this. They want time to work out, hang out with their families and/or significant others, and also meet the demands of their jobs.

You cook. You organize. You coordinate. You nurture. You bring home the bacon and balance the competing demands of work and home. The list continues through the rest of the day and into the evening. By the time you finally sit down at 9 p.m., you are exhausted. You've done everything for everyone else, but you haven't taken time to meet your own needs or to fulfill your own desires.

Exercise? No time. Meditation? Nope, your mind starts to drift immediately. A manicure? Your nails get wrecked when you cook and do dishes anyway—what's the point? A massage? Ha! Travel? A pipe dream!

Stop letting life get away from you and carve out some "me time." Learn how to put yourself first so that you are in an excellent state to take care of the people and things that are important to you. Filling your own tank first allows you to love, enjoy, and care for others in the best way that you can. This is not being selfish. By putting yourself first, you show up as the best version of yourself.

One of my clients, Rich, let himself get way out of shape. The demands of work and business travel (which accounted for 70 percent of his work week) tired him out, and he understandably wanted to spend any spare time he had back home with his family. Rich, though, was not feeling his best. Far from it. He felt exhausted, heavy, and unhealthy, and, as a result, paid little attention to what he ate.

What's the point? Feeling that any effort to make healthier choices was futile, Rich had no motivation to take care of himself.

One day, Rich just had enough. He realized that if he kept going down this path of careless eating and drinking, no exercise, and no down time for himself, he would end up in an ER somewhere. Rich did not want that.

Rich carved out some "me time." Recognizing that spending time with his family whenever he could was the most important thing to him, he began to travel with workout clothes and running shoes, downloaded exercise videos, and started to be more careful about his food and beverage choices. Rich also set a personal goal to run a 10K race within the year. Within months, he dropped a noticeable amount of weight, increased his fitness levels, and had more energy. When he did spend time with his family, Rich could really enjoy his children. He felt like a new man.

What happens when you're hungry, exhausted, or unfulfilled? If you are like most people, you have a shorter fuse and are ill-equipped to listen to the needs and desires of those around you. Maybe you yell more. Or retreat more. Are you any fun? Are you effective at work? I, for one, am definitely less motivational and inspirational when I'm in this state. Only by taking care of myself first can I be of optimal service to others. Use this Sweet Spot Check to catapult yourself to the top of your list. Neither you nor anyone else in your life will be sorry you did.

 SWEET SPOT CHECK **CARVE OUT ME TIME**

- Recognize that you must take care of your own health and well-being first if you want to be your most positive and productive self—at work, at home, or anywhere else. Ask yourself if your current course is sustainable. Are you really giving the best of yourself, or do you feel like you're running on fumes?

- Contemplate what you are putting off in favor of taking care of other people or other things. What will restore your spirit and put you in your sweet spot so that you can be your best self? (For example, it could be exercise, cooking, reading for pleasure, a creative project, yoga, pure relaxation, or anything else that brings you personal happiness.)
- Carve out time for that activity on a weekly, if not a daily, basis. Whether it's a few hours a week or just fifteen minutes a day, make it a regular commitment to yourself. Treat this "me time" with utmost respect.

When the topic of "me time" comes up, so many of my clients say they just don't have the time. They perceive the whole idea as a luxury. However, once they incorporate a personal priority into their schedules and commit to it, they realize that it does in fact make them more effective at work and happier and more patient at home.

For me, exercise is my ultimate "me time" activity. Unless there's some super special occasion, exercise is absolutely nonnegotiable, like brushing my teeth. With a busy schedule that includes taking care of my family, working, writing, traveling, and maintaining a social life, sometimes fitting in exercise requires me to wake up unreasonably early. But when I exercise, I don't think about anything else. I get healthy. I reset. In that moment, I put myself first and get what I

Sweet Spot Tip: Devoting even fifteen minutes every single day to an activity just for you can be surprisingly productive. When you let your mind relax into that space, great ideas often arise. For my clients, the creative thinking that can naturally occur during "me time" has been a source of new business concepts and relationship solutions.

need. This strategy works for me, it works for my clients, and it can work for you.

Make the time. Time is the great democratizer! We all have the same twenty-four hours in the day. What do *you* want to do with them? How can you improve your health, revive your spirit, and feed your soul?

Reboot with the Emergency Redazzle

Ideally, you carve out "me time." You pick the activity, budget the time, and enter it into your calendar. In a perfect world, this appointment with yourself remains nonnegotiable so you can give yourself the juice you need to get through your day. But it doesn't always happen this way. Sometimes even the best-laid plans go completely awry and you find yourself spinning out of control.

Remember when you woke up this morning, gave yourself a little pep talk, and cruised through the first part of your day with relative optimism? Then something happened that diverted you from the rosy path, and everything devolved pretty quickly from there. You know what I mean. Now, you're struggling to get everything done. Work has piled up. Dinner remains uncooked. Your spouse talks at you. Your kids make demands. The doorbell sounds. The phone rings. Everyone seems to want something from you, and you can please no one. It is absolute mayhem, and all you want to do is scream.

Here's where the Emergency Redazzle comes in, and where you step out. When everything is coming apart at the seams and you notice your fuse getting dangerously short (maybe it's already exploded), excuse yourself for ten minutes—or, better yet, twenty—and then do whatever you need to do. Breathe. Meditate. Invoke your mantras. Practice gratitude. Punch a pillow if you have to! No matter where you are in your day, recognize when you need to find your center and then do it.

This happened to me just recently. I was overwhelmed. Being at the helm of two active enterprises (my family and my business) and consistently attempting to have a social life to boot, my schedule can get hectic. Taking charge of all of it, I am the one with all the answers, so everyone comes to me for solutions. The other day, I found myself getting frustrated over the littlest transgressions, my blood on the cusp of boil.

Before I really let someone have it for no good reason, I announced, "No one come into my room. I need twenty minutes to be on my own.

Twenty minutes. Please!" Then I retreated to my bedroom, picked a beautiful guided meditation, and breathed my way back to my center. Deep, cleansing breaths in and toxicity out. I emerged from those twenty minutes in a totally different state. And I'm not the only one who felt the difference. My husband and my children appreciated my transformation almost as much as I did. Twenty minutes of the Emergency Redazzle, and I was fine.

Here's your own emergency tool kit to use when you need it.

 SWEET SPOT CHECK   **EMERGENCY REDAZZLE**

- **Recognize the moments when you need to rejigger your energy. Notice the early signs (e.g., making verbal swipes, feeling your breath quicken, swearing under your breath) so you can nip anything worse in the bud.**
- **As soon as you feel yourself losing your cool, give yourself a time-out and retreat to a space where you will be undisturbed. This space can be a bathroom, a backyard, or even a city street. You just need to step away from the frenetic environment that's causing you to spiral.**
- **Choose an activity that will change your energy flow. You can go for a quick walk, do jumping jacks, dance around your bathroom, take a shower, or even just take deep, cleansing breaths. Work the unproductive energy out of your system until you feel the sea change inside of you.**
- **Reemerge and share your redazzled self!**

When you feel yourself getting overwhelmed, allow yourself the possibility that you're not being your best self and then take the emergency action to rectify it. There's no shame in it (it happens to all of us), but there's no need to announce it or alarm anyone, either. Just take the time to recenter yourself, and then move on with your life.

Cherish Sleep

Susan Cross, my trusted holistic health counselor and dear friend, taught me that sleep is a fundamental part of weight management and metabolic maintenance. In fact, she says that if you want to impact your metabolism positively, sleep more. Another bonus is that, apart from rigorous exercise, sleep is the other known source of HGH, the hormone that keeps you young. Pretty cool, right?

Here's something else to consider. In *Brain Rules*, molecular biologist John Medina shares a compelling bit of research: "When sleep was restricted to six hours or less per night for just five nights, for example, cognitive performance matched that of a person suffering from forty-eight hours of continual sleep deprivation" (p. 162). Makes you think twice about taking on the night shift, doesn't it? Now imagine trying to make an important decision, balance your checkbook, or pay attention at a work meeting without having slept for forty-eight hours. Imagine your mood, your mindset, your productivity.

I know it can be hard to get enough sleep—there's always something on TV, a social commitment, or the need to catch up on work. Last night, I found myself tapping out e-mails at 12:43 a.m. when my ideal goal for lights-out is 10:30 p.m. Ensuring that you get enough sleep can be hard to execute, but it comes with tremendous benefits. Quite simply, sleep is a prerequisite for functioning in your sweet spot. Getting sufficient sleep is part of filling your own tank *first*.

One of my clients, Rhonda, worked a lot and slept little. She woke at 4 a.m. in order to get three hours of uninterrupted work in before she headed in to the office. She then cranked hard at work, stopping only briefly for fuel (read: coffee) every few hours, staying at the office until 10 p.m. Then she went home, wound down, and collapsed in bed, only to rise again at 4 a.m.

By the second half of the week, Rhonda was exhausted, less focused, and less patient with her colleagues. Before we began our work together, she was becoming ineffective—terse with her direct reports and annoyed with her CEO. In fact, Rhonda was becoming so short-tempered at work that her colleagues began to avoid her, making her team unproductive. The big boss began to take note and almost let Rhonda go, even though she was an integral part of the business. Moreover, annoying health issues began to crop up.

Although Rhonda started her weeks following a pretty nutritious regimen, by Thursday evening, she would reach for anything and everything—at 10 or 11 p.m., just before going to bed. The cookie jar always seemed like a good idea. More accurately, she would polish off the cookies before she even had a chance to think about whether she wanted them in the first place. But she deserved them, dammit, as hard as she was working!

During our work together, Rhonda realized she had to change her sleep habits. There was no way she was treating her body right on four hours of sleep a night, her declining job performance aside. Here's what Rhonda did that may help you, too.

 SWEET SPOT CHECK   **CHERISH SLEEP**

- **Keep a sleep log for a week. Note what time you go to sleep and what time you wake. Tally up the hours for each night. Are you getting less than seven or eight hours a night?**
- **Take note of your usual evening routine before bed. If you spend a significant amount of time watching TV or surfing the Internet, set an earlier time for punching out of these activities at the end of the day.**
- **Pick a quiet activity that you love but that will help you wind down. It could be reading, writing, crafting, or enjoying a quiet conversation with your significant other.**
- **Set an earlier time for getting into bed, and adhere to it consistently every night. Doing a meditation, deep breathing, or a gratitude practice can help you fall asleep.**

It won't take long for your body to adapt to your new sleep schedule. Since you will be getting more ZZZs on the front end, you should be able to rise and shine at the same hour as before, if not a bit earlier.

Did this have an impact on Rhonda's routine? Absolutely. She became more productive and focused, even with fewer working hours each week. Her colleagues, responding to her more pleasant disposition, were willing to collaborate and pick up many of the assignments she had taken on herself. People remembered why they liked this competent colleague. A sense of teamwork prevailed. On the personal front, Rhonda began losing weight and enjoying regular nutritious meals. No more 11 p.m. cookie jar binges.

Sleep—it's the overlooked elixir. At first blush, you may not think you can sacrifice any of those waking hours, but if you aren't getting sufficient sleep, you can and you must find the time for it. Look carefully and mercilessly at how you're spending those late-night hours. Find a better way to wind down. Trust me. Even a fraction of an hour more sleep each night can make a world of difference, giving you that extra bit of juice you need to sweeten your days.

Rise and Shine

Yes, sufficient sleep is critical to your sweet spot. But if you combine that with getting up earlier, you can add monumental productivity to your day. Take advantage of those quiet moments in the morning before your hectic day begins to ensure that you find time for what you love. Here are some things that clients tell me they do when they wake up just thirty minutes earlier than usual:

- Have a quiet cup of tea.
- Read the paper with no distractions.
- Meditate.
- Exercise.
- Prepare and eat a hearty and healthy breakfast.
- Take a brisk walk.
- Snuggle.
- Chat with the kids without feeling rushed.
- Clean up e-mails that have sat in the inbox forever.
- Keep a gratitude journal.

Ever have one those days where you fully intend to make time for a special activity in the evening, but something gets in the way? Exhaustion, drinks with colleagues, a phone call, errands, laziness, TV, social media, unexpected work? Do any or all of the above ring true for you? What can you do to avoid those detours and distractions? Get up early. Get that activity into your day before your brain gives you excuses not to. Yes, it is that simple. Don't give yourself an out.

My killer app in the morning is exercise, but if I don't get it in by 10 a.m., my opportunity is shot. I just don't do it. It's as if I'm allergic to afternoon workouts! Nevertheless, I still have days when the blare of the alarm sounds impossible and the snooze button beckons. However, I know that my morning routine will get my blood pumping and set me up beautifully for the rest of the day. It's a glorious feeling to emerge from a spin class at 7 a.m. bubbling with positive energy, and have the whole day to look forward to.

What will motivate you to get up and out of bed and ensure that you start your day off right? A morning run? A guided meditation? Reading the paper? You don't have to get up at the crack of dawn, and you don't even have to be a "morning person" per se to make the following Sweet Spot Check work for you. Just choose an activity that truly inspires you and that you can consistently make time for at the beginning of your day.

 SWEET SPOT CHECK **RISE AND SHINE**

- **Begin with the Cherish Sleep Sweet Spot Check from the previous chapter. Waking up earlier will benefit you only if you're getting to bed earlier and/or getting sufficient sleep.**
- **Have a specific purpose for waking up. It can be anything that will inspire you to get out of bed and set you up for a productive day. You can think of this as "me time"—a way to feed your soul before the rest of the day's demands come barging in. If it helps to have some accountability, sign up for a class or choose an activity you can enjoy with a friend.**
- **Plan out how much extra time you will need for it in the morning and set your alarm accordingly. Send yourself a wake-up message that inspires you to rise and shine.**
- **Once the alarm goes off, get up! Remind yourself of the morning's special purpose. Don't give yourself any other option. It's much less painful just to get up than to keep hitting snooze. Before long, your body will adjust to the**

earlier wake-up call, and the benefits of your new morning routine will reinforce your commitment.

As long as you get enough sleep at night, you'll love having this extra time to yourself in the morning. Choose an activity that enthuses you and let it infuse the rest of your day with sweetness. Rise and shine!

Have Fun

Many of us get so focused on everything we need to get done that we often forget the importance of having fun. Fun becomes a total afterthought. But fun is essential to our lives. It's not a bonus. Laughter, play, enjoyment, joy—these are the experiences that keep us young and in our sweet spot. But yes, finding room for fun in our busy schedules can be a challenge. In fact, having to schedule time for fun sometimes takes the fun out of it, doesn't it?

One week in Honolulu, my daughter, Sloane, wanted to give an aqua cycle a whirl along the ocean. Although I grew up in Hawaii and love looking at the water, I sometimes find getting *into* the water to be more pain than joy . . . wet hair, salty skin, extra SPF, plus the drive through touristy Waikiki and having to stake out a spot on the sand. (Did I just admit that?) Hence, the aqua cycle did not top my list of things to do.

Well, this day, I decided not to let the palaver get in the way. I drove my kids to Waikiki, found parking (easier than I'd anticipated), and got us to the beach. I rented an aqua cycle and we all got on—Sloane, Finn, and me. Guess what? We all *loved* it. What a treat for the three of us to be out on the water together looking back at Diamond Head and the beach landscape. The kids oohed and ahhed, and I, too, marveled at the beauty of this place where I grew up. We giggled and screamed as we pedaled our hearts out. Fun? Check that bad boy off my list!

But then, after we disembarked, my resistance to play set in again immediately when Sloane asked me to go for a swim with her. Ugh, didn't we just have fun with the aqua cycle? I was on a schedule with many preflight errands to run, so my initial response was, "No, we don't have time—we have to leave soon." And then there were the obstacles in my head: *I don't want to drive in a wet bathing suit. . . . I don't want to get salty. . . . I'm much too full from lunch to be strutting in a bikini. . . .*

Then I caught myself. I was just making excuses, being the staid grown-up. *Okay*, I thought, *let's have fun!* I stripped off my cover-up and plunged into the water. Sloane, erupting in laughter and palpable joy, came rushing in after me. Not only were we having fun, but we were bonding and creating the kind of memories that would sustain us as a family for years to come.

Of course, fun comes much more naturally to children, before life heaps a bunch of responsibilities on them. As adults, we sometimes need to make a more conscious effort to get in the spirit of fun and make it happen. That's why I ask my clients what they do for fun. Here is a sampling of activities my clients have enjoyed over the last year, along with a few of my favorites too. These fun activities have brought us unfailing joy and put us right in our sweet spot!

- zip-lining
- paddleboarding
- rock climbing
- dancing
- rollerblading
- jet skiing
- trapeze lessons
- horseback riding
- singing in a choir
- girls' night out
- book club
- cooking
- fishing
- running
- crafting with friends

Now it's your turn to have fun. Develop a passion for playtime with this Sweet Spot Check.

- What do you do for fun? Think of all the things you do in your current life for sheer joy and amusement. Is there enough fun in your life? Do you laugh and play and feel young on a regular basis? (My guess is, probably not often enough!)

- What fun activities would you like to sample or enjoy more often? Don't think about any of the logistics yet. Just imagine the activities that would bring you the greatest joy and happiness.

- Now weigh the effort of pursuing each of these activities against the sheer enjoyment you would experience doing them. When you find one or two that tip the scales toward enjoyment, and where you might even enjoy the preparations involved, commit to making it happen.

- Carve out the time for this activity. Whether it's a one-off excursion or more of a regular commitment, plan for it and enter it into your calendar. Then look forward to it!

- When the time comes, summon your inner child and throw yourself into it, whole hog. Set aside all your worldly concerns and just have fun!

- Keep your mind open to the spirit of fun even when you're not doing your scheduled activity. Opportunities for fun can arise in almost any context, even in the middle of your work day. Have a laugh. Be spontaneous. Do something out of the ordinary. Those brief moments of fun will bring a touch of levity and optimism to your day.

Once you're out on the proverbial aqua cycle, you will completely forget the hassles of getting there. You'll just remember the joy and freedom of having fun. Stop missing out, and get out there!

Say It Loud!

Once your goals are crystallized in your mind's eye, once you have a clear vision of your star and you've seen it done, how do you hold yourself accountable for actually taking the steps to get there? You say it *out loud*. Whatever your dream or goal, you make it that much more real by declaring it to someone else.

When I decided to train for a half marathon, I thought I'd keep the training to myself. After all, what if I didn't make it? But then I realized that if I let people know what I was doing, I would have others to hold me accountable as well as to support me through the process. I also realized that I could use this personal challenge as a tool to help others accomplish their "nevers," since a long race was certainly one of mine. So I talked about it with friends. I wrote about it on my blog. I wanted accountability and got it.

Even though I had the strength of my own conviction, I still experienced moments of *Oh dear God, what am I doing?* And in the week leading up to the race: *Hmmm, maybe I'll get lucky and twist my ankle.* In those sinking moments, I had a whole village of friends and colleagues to buoy my strength and determination.

As a bonus, while I trained, my supporters regaled me with their own inspirational running experiences—how they'd overcome injuries and their own self-doubt. I loved hearing their stories and bonding over this community event. I had people e-mailing, texting, and calling me to wish me luck on the race, to tell me how much

Sweet Spot Tip: Have a visible reminder of your strength and objectives. I wear a necklace that reminds me, daily, of all that I've accomplished and of all the support that I have to keep moving forward with confidence. Put up a note. Write on your mirror. Wear a string on your wrist. Use anything that will signify to you—and only you—commitment, motivation, and perseverance.

they believed I could do it. My friends on Facebook cheered. I even had a whole yoga class in Connecticut om-ing for me that Saturday morning!

All of my clients have remarked that speaking their goals out loud has played a large role in realizing their achievements. By sharing their ambitions, they have effectively put a stake in the ground and announced the start of their journeys.

One client, Shane, a father, husband, and executive, struggled to determine what he wanted his next step to be and what he actually wanted out of his life. For years, Shane had worked at the same company, doing work that he enjoyed, but he felt a little unsettled. Perhaps he ought to experience a different corporate culture. Perhaps he needed to ask for a new job, or for a raise. Maybe all he needed was to spend more time with his family. He just couldn't seem to peg what he wanted. Over the course of some coaching sessions, we dug deeper to identify Shane's core values and his goals for himself and for his family. Because he was unsure of where he wanted to end up professionally, he was very reluctant to say anything out loud to anyone.

When I asked him some of the questions that I've shared with you in previous Sweet Spot Checks above, Shane finally figured it out. First he said it out loud to me. Then he called his mentor. He described his newly minted professional vision and then asked for advice on how to manifest it. After a few more calls, Shane's mentor made important introductions for him and set up a number of meetings. Because Shane spoke up, his mentor was happy to help him navigate his next steps. Before long, Shane ended up in the job (via an internal promotion) that matched his vision—an excellent outcome.

Sweet Spot Tip: Find an accountability buddy. Checking in regularly—weekly, or even daily—with a friend is a great way to keep yourself on track to your star. You can support each other's journeys through the difficult patches and then celebrate the wins, big and small!

Now it's your turn. Say your goals out loud. See how much support you can garner around you. Articulating your aspirations, and having others to hold you accountable to them, are giant steps toward manifesting your star. Here's how.

 SWEET SPOT CHECK **SAY IT LOUD!**

- Once you have a clear vision of your star and you've seen it done, write it down. (At this juncture, it may help you to look at your cut-out star from the Shape Your Star Sweet Spot Check and to review your notes from the See It Done Sweet Spot Check.) By seeing what you wish to accomplish in words, you can hold *yourself* accountable.

- Now that you've clarified your goal to yourself, say it out loud to someone whom you trust to be supportive and to provide constructive feedback. Whether you share it with a friend, a coach, a family member, or a mentor, saying it out loud makes your goal even more concrete. It is also a good test of the strength of your vision. Now that you've shared it out loud, does it still sound right to you? Could it be clarified or strengthened in any way?

- Then, according to your comfort level, share your goal with others. Start with your most trusted allies and then reach out to your wider community. If you wish, post your star on your social media pages and see the responses you get. You might even start a blog to capture your journey.

- Keep your "star village" updated on your progress. The more you talk about your star, the clearer and brighter it will shine, and the closer you will get to making it a reality.

- Solicit advice or help in manifesting your star. People are honored to be asked for advice, and you never know who will be happy to extend a helping hand. Inviting others to

take part in your journey can foster a sense of community and bring mutual fulfillment. (Can you recall a time you helped someone else reach his or her goal, and how good that felt?)
• Once you reach your goal, show your gratitude and celebrate with the people who've supported you!

Don't try to go it alone. Sometimes it does take a village to manifest a star. Garner the support you'll need to push through any obstacles, setbacks, or moments of self-doubt. Learn from other people's stories and experiences. Invite them to be a part of your exciting journey. Be careful, though, of announcing your goal and not following through. Strive to be worthy of their steadfast love and support!

Assemble Your Star Village

Daniel Goleman, PhD, author of *Emotional Intelligence*, posits that "emotions are contagious." He describes the way people mirror one another to "re-create in themselves the mood of the other person" (p. 115). If this is the case, then we want to make sure that we are in excellent company! We need people in our lives who will celebrate our wins and believe in our dreams and for whom we can do the same. We also need to be around people who inspire us and keep our standards high. With this in mind, build your star village.

One recent fall, a few of my girlfriends came from faraway places to reconnect in New York City. The four of us spent the weekend laughing, shopping, and talking about our wins, our life challenges, and our goals. One thing that we all wanted was to feel better and more fit day to day. We also expressed a desire to keep growing in our careers, as well as in our personal lives.

Sweet Spot Tip: Get to know your friends—who they are as well as what they can do—and let them get to know you in the same way. You may think you already know your friends' skills and talents, but if you dig a little deeper, you might be surprised. Also, deeper conversations can shine a light on hidden dreams and unspoken ambitions. Find new ways of supporting one other.

As a result of this weekend, we all went back to our lives determined to pursue the goals we had talked about, and to support one another in the process. Here is a sampling of our various action items: exercise, begin writing a book, activate a dating strategy, have an honest conversation with a significant other, stop dating duds, sign up to run a marathon, adopt a healthier nutrition plan. All of these things would require individual effort, for sure, but they would also require the group's support and some level of accountability, which we each agreed to provide.

The great thing about these girlfriends is that I have tremendous respect for them. They inspire me to aspire to more because they want the best for themselves and for me. None of us is perfect; nor do we claim to be. Our one-on-one relationships are incredibly productive, so imagine the strength of the collective group! Think about it this way: You can break a single chopstick with no problem. You could probably do it with one hand. But imagine trying to break a handful of chopsticks. Not so easy. Humans, too, are much stronger by the handful.

Assemble your star village. Populate it wisely so that you consistently inspire one another to work toward your stars. Consider which friends are helping or hindering your journey. Who is positive and inspiring? Who may be holding you back or lowering your standards with negativity? Be honest with yourself.

 SWEET SPOT CHECK **ASSEMBLE YOUR STAR VILLAGE**

- Consider the people around you—both in your immediate physical environment and in your wider community (online and offline). How do you support these people in their lives, and how do they do the same for you? Think about family, friends, colleagues, acquaintances, and fellow community members—the whole constellation of people who make up your world.
- Who among them would qualify for a position in your star village? Whom do you find most inspiring, supportive, and positive? Who fills your heart with love and reflects your best self back to you? Who among them would gladly share in your dreams, and ask you to share in theirs? Most likely, you will want to choose individuals from your close circle of friends and family, but there may be colleagues or others who fit the bill.

- Are there friends or family members who make it diffi-cult for you to keep moving toward your star? Naysay-ers, perhaps? Individuals who bring you down with their negativity and lack of faith? If there are, love them still, but insert a bit of distance between you and them to give yourself the positive space you need to grow—and to free up more time for the people who truly support and inspire you.
- Seek out regular and meaningful connections with those individuals who will support you and hold you account-able. If you can't meet in person (the ideal way to meet), connect by phone, e-mail, video calls, or instant mes-saging. Show your gratitude regularly and remember to reciprocate the inspiration and support.
- Celebrate the wins, big and little, with all the members of your star village!

Now, if you don't already enjoy a social life and a sense of com-munity, you may find it difficult to build a star village. Creating meaningful friendships requires attention and effort, especially as we get older and more settled in our ways. As Csikszentmihalyi, world-renowned psychologist and researcher on positive psychology, points out in *Flow*, "Friendships rarely happen by chance: one must culti-vate them as assiduously as one must cultivate a job or a family" (pp. 189–90).

If you, like many adults, feel a lack of community, make the effort to cultivate one. Create opportunities to meet new friends and strengthen bonds with old ones. Friendships take time, care, and attention. This may sound elementary, but in the busyness of our modern lives, we can lose sight of this fact. If you are finding it difficult to assemble your star village, do this Sweet Spot Check to cultivate friendships and a sense of community.

SWEET SPOT CHECK **CULTIVATE COMMUNITY**

- **Start with the people with whom you're already familiar.** Resurrect your relationships with old buddies of whom you may have lost sight along the way. Reach out to them with a friendly message or (gasp!) pick up the phone.
- **Really commit.** If you want to make your friendships and community a priority, commit to a certain number of meet-ups each week. Whether it's in a group or one-on-one, a lunch or a night out, or even just a ten-minute visit, stick with the assiduous effort.
- **Whip up social media.** If you are active on social media of any kind, you probably know your friends and acquaintances better than you did before. If there's someone you feel a special connection with online, take it offline. Video chat if you live far apart; otherwise, meet over coffee.
- **Seize and create opportunities to meet new friends.** Attend company happy hours. Volunteer at your children's school. Take a class that interests you. Join a group fitness class or a book club. The more you show up, the easier it will be to turn these early acquaintances into more meaningful friendships.
- **Rally.** Yes, there will be times when you've made plans and it is oh-so-tempting (and now, with technology, oh-so-easy) to bail. You don't feel like getting dressed up. You'd rather stay home to watch the game. Don't. By bailing, you'll miss an opportunity to connect, and make it that much easier to bail the next time. As Woody Allen once said, "Eighty percent of success is showing up."

Your star village can be small and powerful, or you can seek a mutually supportive rapport with a flock of many. It's up to you how you want to create it.

Get a Coach

This is not a plug for me or for the coaching industry. I honestly believe that everyone—every single one of us—can benefit tremendously from a coach.

I have a coach. In my sessions, I can be 100 percent comfortable and honest with Sharon, knowing that she has no personal agenda in my life that might taint her views. Friends and family with the best intentions can't offer the same impartiality, which is why coaches are ethically bound *not* to coach close relations. My coach provides insights that would otherwise elude me, due to certain blind spots, habits, and perspectives I've held for my entire life. In other words, she can cut through the BS with razor-sharp precision.

A coach can help you to find your sweet spot by asking probing questions, listening objectively, sharing insights, offering concrete advice when called for, assisting you to create action steps toward your goals, holding you accountable, encouraging you through the challenges, and celebrating your wins with you. I have witnessed profound progress, complete transformation even, in people's lives because of their work with coaches. Here are some examples from my own coaching practice:

- Wyatt attained a highly sought-after position—a medical fellowship—that he thought others would easily beat him on, and which posed familial and geographical obstacles. He worked it all out, achieved this win, and now enjoys a renewed love for his career.
- Helen discarded old beliefs that she "wasn't good enough" and stepped up her game significantly, fully owning the power of the position she held and impressing her colleagues and clients.
- Frank, a high-achieving executive, stopped being overly self-deprecating and diminishing his accomplishments to others. This allowed him to take more pride in his work (while letting

184

others recognize it too) and achieve an even greater level of excellence.

- After months of sitting around and waiting for things to happen for her, Shelley actively pursued her dream job in another country, got it, and started a new life in a cool city.
- Daryl stopped lamenting what he characterized as an ill-conceived career move, honed his interviewing skills, targeted new companies, and, despite a couple of setbacks, landed the job in which he felt he really belonged. To boot, he was thrilled to relocate his family to a fantastic family-friendly city.
- While still working at her day job, Stella started a business that nurtured and fueled her passion—helping others achieve health and fitness.
- Tammy worked through difficult relationships that had been crushing her productivity and performance at work by looking at them from an entirely different perspective.
- Timothy stopped beating himself up for the unlovable and unattractive person that he thought he was and developed a beautiful relationship, the kind that had eluded him for years.

With a coach, these individuals were able to identify their strengths and weaknesses as well as their aspirations. They created new beliefs and new visions. They began approaching their lives differently. Every one of them made significant progress toward his or her goals, often achieving them more quickly than they'd anticipated. Week after week, they had a coach to hold them accountable to their plans and troubleshoot with them to find solutions to challenges.

Sweet Spot Tip: Take advantage of the complimentary coaching session that most coaches offer. For a successful coaching relationship, you must like and respect your coach and be open to his or her process. No two coaches are exactly alike, so be sure to find one who connects well with you and understands your needs.

In a confidential setting, coaching clients get to let their hair down, without fear of being judged, offending others, or not being heard. With no other agenda than to help the client, the coach can provide genuine support and encouragement to keep the client moving toward his or her star. Best of all, the coach has a vested interest in the client's wins, so there is frequent and genuine cause for celebration! Use this Sweet Spot Check to see if you need a coach.

 SPOT CHECK **GET A COACH**

- Can you identify a dream or a set of goals that you'd like to achieve, but you've noticed you lack the motivation, know-how, or follow-through to get there?
- What is a specific behavior, whether work-related or more personal, that you'd like to change?
- What's something in your current situation that you'd like to change, but you can't figure out how or can't find the courage to take action?
- What issues might you like to discuss about your work or your personal life, but you worry about offending others or being judged? Do you crave sound, objective advice from someone who has no personal stake in your life?
- How might you like to be able to express yourself more clearly, whether in one-on-one conversations or in public speaking situations?
- Do you feel that your life is pretty good, but you want to keep evolving and reaching new levels of excellence?

A skilled coach can help you with any or all of the above, targeting various facets of your life. I absolutely love the progress I'm able to make with my coach's support, as well as the lightbulb moments I experience because she's reading out of a different songbook. Thanks in large part to my coach, I have built a bigger business, written a book, overcome bumps in my marriage, found the strength to be a more patient mother, and continue to clean up my nutrition. I am so grateful. Sitting on the other side of the desk as a coach, I get a huge kick out of witnessing real and positive transformation in the lives of my clients. It gives me profound pleasure to be able to help someone climb out of a difficult place and fulfill his or her potential. I am so grateful to be on both sides of this dynamic equation.

See what you can accomplish with the help of a coach!

Transfer Your Skills

Everyone is good at *something*. Yes, even if you feel that you are not particularly skilled at anything useful, you *are* good at something. Dig deep and figure out what that is, whether it's applicable to work or to your family or to just going about your daily routines. There is something valuable there.

On the flip side of the same coin, we all have areas of difficulty. There are things that don't come naturally to us. Here's the trick: Transfer the skills you have on Easy Street to those more difficult areas.

What do I mean? Take Maria's story. Maria is an athlete. Six mornings a week, she wakes early without issue to ensure that she gets her daily sweat on. No negotiation with the alarm clock. She just pops out of bed. As a result, Maria is in excellent health and, at age forty-six, she has a body most twenty-two-year-olds would die for. No doubt, Maria excels at health and fitness.

What was her area of difficulty? Organizing her life. Maria constantly overbooked and under-delivered. She often missed appointments or scrambled at the last minute to get there, causing her unnecessary stress. She let bills pile up for weeks, then opened them all at once, often sending in checks past the due date. More unnecessary stress.

Our solution? Maria would approach her life in the same way she approached exercise—with focus and consistency for at least one hour a day. She'd transfer the same skills that allowed her to excel at exercise to her admin tasks. At first, Maria resisted. She couldn't fathom sitting for an hour at her desk just to organize her calendar and attend to paperwork. It didn't compute.

Reluctantly, Maria carved out an hour a day for organization, right after her usual exercise, shower, and breakfast. This way, her admin tasks almost became an extension of her workout routine. Since she'd worked hard to be disciplined about waking up for the gym each day for so many years, her daily habit was etched deeply into her brain. Adding another hour after her regular exercise? A walk in the park.

Now, Maria dedicates an hour each day to organizing her calendar (and that of her children), opening mail, paying bills, and taking care of the regular administration that consumes any head of household. Her life has done a 180—she's no longer frazzled, stressed, and frantic. She enjoys a level of calm in her routine that she hadn't thought possible, simply by applying her exercise habits to her home administration.

Another scenario: Madison was perennially confident and at ease in business situations. She knew what to do, what to say, and how it all must come together. When she walked into any work situation, her body language exuded confidence, her thoughts were organized, and her execution was fluid. As a result, Madison's successes had piled up and she enjoyed a lucrative career.

Where Madison had struggled, however, was in her personal life. While she was supremely adept in the boardroom, she couldn't seem to find that sweet spot in personal relationships. While she could stride confidently into any work setting, Madison got visibly nervous in social situations. Her body language immediately gave her away. She'd start to fidget and her brain would revert to unproductive thoughts: *Oh my God, he can tell I'm nervous. He'll never find me attractive. Why can't I just talk to him like a normal human being?*

When, with some questioning, Madison noticed the difference between her confident approach in work situations and her unease outside them, she realized she had been sabotaging her own opportunities to connect with others. Madison also realized that after years of honing her communication skills at work, she could begin to apply what she'd mastered there to her personal life. She created mantras to bolster her confidence in social settings, sweetened her beliefs about herself, and then got herself out there to meet new people. By channeling her confidence from her work persona into her personal interactions, Madison found that she could connect with people with greater ease and build more fulfilling relationships.

What are your transferable skills? Use this Sweet Spot Check to find out and start putting them to use.

 SWEET SPOT CHECK   **TRANSFER YOUR SKILLS**

- Identify an area of your life that comes very easily to you. Identify the skills that allow you to occupy this part of your life with excellence and ease.
- On the other hand, identify another area of your life that you find challenging and that needs improvement.
- Identify the similarities and differences between those two areas, paying special attention to where they overlap.
- Identify the specific skills and strengths that you routinely bring to the first that might be transferable to the other.
- Apply those skills to the more difficult area of your life and notice the difference.

Capitalize on familiar skills that are already in your wheelhouse. Implement them in other areas of your life and let them lead you to excellence.

Chunk It Up

It's very easy to get overwhelmed by the sheer length of our to-do lists. We look at our frantic lives, filled with obligations and endless responsibilities, and we get overwhelmed. Here's a suggestion: Chunk it up. What does that mean? It means bite off no more than you can chew at a time. Break up an enormous challenge into smaller, more palatable bits.

I discovered the utility of this approach during a really arduous workout at the gym. My trainer switched up my sessions and infused eight über-intense one-minute intervals into my one-hour session. Eight minutes might not sound like a lot, and I was only doing them one minute at a time, but at points during these intervals, running as hard as I could on a steep incline, I had genuine fear that my lungs would give out on me—or that I'd just fall flat on my face.

These sixty-second intervals were so challenging that I had to talk myself through the anxiety and the physical act. At one point, I found myself saying, *I can do this. Easy! Only three more intervals. Just three more minutes . . . Wait! Three minutes?!* When I'm running that hard, even three minutes is a helluva long time. Anxiety. Doubt. I started to feel sick to my stomach.

At that moment, with three minutes to go, I realized I had to chunk it up. Instead of thinking of the total remaining minutes, I focused solely on the task at hand: *I can do this. Just one minute.* I knew that to think any further into the future (even two measly minutes into the future) would only increase my anxiety and threaten to obliterate any belief that I could finish. So, instead, I resolved to run my hardest just for that one interval, and worry about crossing the next bridge only when I came to it. Staying in the moment, right then and there, quelled my anxiety. Three more minutes was too much for me to handle. One minute—*that* I could do.

You can apply this scary intervals scenario to anything you do. Take an overwhelming challenge or your long to-do list and break it down into smaller chunks or intervals. Focus on what you can take care of now, leaving the rest for when you get to them. Don't even think about the magnitude of the entire challenge. Instead, use the following Sweet Spot Check to simplify it.

SWEET SPOT CHECK **CHUNK IT UP**

Each person's gargantuan challenges will look different. Use the strategies in the following examples as a basic blueprint to chunk up whatever intimidating, sizable challenge you may encounter into smaller, easier tasks:

- *You are applying for a new job.* There is your résumé to prepare, research to conduct, informational meetings to schedule, cover letters to write, recommendations to collect, interview outfits to coordinate . . . you know the drill. On top of the logistics, just the idea of searching for a job is unsettling, so taken all together, this is an enormous source of stress. Before you start to panic, take a deep breath and chunk it up. Take it on bit by bit. Start with the first task and forget the rest. Then move on to the second task—again, without worrying about the rest. And so on, and so forth. Have faith that at any given time, you are moving in the right direction.

- *You are tired of being overweight and you want to lose ten pounds.* Instead of focusing on those ten pounds, focus on losing one pound first. Instead of trying to implement changes across the board all at once (scary!), commit to making one change in the coming week, whether it's dietary or exercise-related. Maybe that means signing up for one extra cardio blast class. Or reducing your dessert intake from three to one per week. Just take one step. Make it your goal to lose one pound in the next week. There, that's one chunk. Worry about next week (and the next pound) when you get to it.

- *Your relationship with your partner has been in the doldrums.* Instead of focusing on all the things that you find annoying about your partner, and all the ways that your relationship falls short of your ideal, do one small thing a day that will enhance your connection. Smile at your partner in the morning. Ask your partner how the day went. Send a text just to say hello. Go on a dinner date. Schedule sex—and then have it! Remind yourself and each other moment by moment, day by day, why you love each other. Use a succession of thoughtful words and actions to rekindle the passion. They don't all have to be grand gestures or happen all at once.
- *You're writing an important report.* Just thinking about it causes heart palpitations! Breathe. The beauty of having to write anything is that you can literally chunk it up into sections, pages, paragraphs, or sentences—whatever size chunks are the most productive for you. Create a working outline and tackle one section at a time. Don't think about the number of pages you have left to write—focus on the page you're on.

You can chunk up anything in your life that threatens to overwhelm or squash your spirit. It's a surefire method of making a giant project more manageable and much less stressful. The trick is to focus on that one little step that creates movement in the right direction, which, in turn, motivates you to take the next one.

Serve Your Community

An effective way to stay in your sweet spot that is often overlooked is to serve your community. By helping others, you gain perspective, feel useful, and improve lives—superb nourishment for your sweet spot.

Jessica Mindich is a New York jewelry designer who found her sweet spot by coming up with a brilliant way to give back to her community: designing beautiful jewelry made out of repurposed metals from a massive stockpile of weapons that had been returned to Newark, New Jersey, police departments as part of a no-questions-asked gun buyback program. With proceeds from the sale of these fabulous bracelets, the Caliber Collection, Jessica provides beleaguered governments with extra funds. Her work is so meaningful that governments and police departments from other cities and even countries have contacted her to inquire about doing the same for them. Jessica has successfully combined her talents in business with her passion for jewelry to serve her community. Sweet spot city!

Sweet Spot Tip: You don't have to be rich or especially privileged to serve your community. If you don't have a lot of time or money to donate, contribute in whatever way you can on a weekly or event basis. There are so many excellent charities out there that are doing important work and that need your help.

I serve on the board of the New York Asian Women's Center (NYAWC), an organization that provides refuge, recovery, and renewal for women and children who are survivors of domestic violence and human trafficking. Between my family, my work, and the activities I maintain to live in my sweet spot, I don't have a lot of extra time. But I find the time to contribute to NYAWC because I know I can make a difference in the lives of people who need support—*and* because it brings me a sense of fulfillment. I love it.

Many of my friends and clients share their time and money with a variety of worthy causes. Contributing your time, your expertise, and your passion to something that you believe in can put you smack-dab in the middle of your sweet spot. It allows you to exercise your natural talents and skills because, as a volunteer, you have the luxury of choosing in what capacity you will serve. Moreover, it's a great way to explore new areas of interest, open your mind to new perspectives, and perhaps even discover a new career path. You get as much as you give, if not more. What are you doing to make the world a better place? What talents, skills, or passions could you contribute to your community? How could a cause you believe in benefit from your time and attention? Do this Sweet Spot Check and find out.

 SWEET SPOT CHECK   **SERVE YOUR COMMUNITY**

- Figure out what need in your community you could help to fill using your innate skills and talents.
- Choose a charity, school, or other not-for-profit organization to which you would be happy dedicating your time. Also, do some research to make sure this organization will make the best use of your time.
- Determine exactly how much time you would be willing to devote to serving your community. Be honest with yourself. Don't overcommit and then find yourself having to cancel or skip appointments. Start with what's manageable, and then you can increase your time commitment as you feel comfortable doing so.
- Keep your commitment and approach the effort responsibly. Just because you aren't getting paid for this work doesn't mean it does not deserve your full attention. Don't be afraid to offer and ask for feedback. Others will appreciate your interest and engagement.
- Feel good about your contributions!

Make Failure a Friend

We can be armed to the hilt with all the sweet spot strategies in the world, and there will still be times when we fail. There will be times when we're tempted to toss everything we've learned out the window, revert to old self-defeating beliefs, and give up on excellence: *I'm such a failure. Why did I think I could to this? Things will never get better. I surrender.* In these moments, it's easy to repudiate the idea of a sweet spot and resign ourselves to "just okay." Failure hurts, and our instinct is often to clam up and protect ourselves from further hurt.

Despite our best efforts, life is not always sunshine and roses. That's just not how life works. Some days are easy and issue-free while others take the wind out of our sails. What's particularly hard is when we have a string of days—weeks or months, even—that feel like one big, never-ending failure. When that happens, it's easy to lose sight of what we are grateful for and only notice the mud, the exhaustion, the failure.

What do you do? You can face failure head-on and learn from it. In *Mindset*, Carol S. Dweck, PhD, puts it this way: "Failure can be a painful experience. But it doesn't define you. It's a problem to be faced, dealt with, and learned from." In other words, failing does not make you a failure.

Failure can be incredibly useful in thinking about how to move forward. In fact, if you use failure as a learning tool, it is no longer a loss but an asset! One of my favorite people in this world has endured the hardest couple of years in his life. In the short span of two and a half years, Jeremy lost his job, divorced, and struggled to pay his bills. The business he started failed, and he faced issues with his health. Nevertheless, Jeremy is able to get up every day and rise to meet the day's challenges. He remains one of the most inspiring and optimistic people I know.

Many of us might have just crawled under the covers and waited for the world to change. But Jeremy, even in his darkest periods, looked at his situation and asked himself, *What am I supposed to be learning here?* Instead of feeling sorry for himself, he looked at every circumstance he'd faced as a lesson. And, despite the scary news he received from his doctor, he found glimmers of hope and maintained a positive attitude throughout the challenges. Jeremy kept his eye on what he wanted to achieve, took steps to improve his health, and just kept plugging with the mantra that *tomorrow will be better.*

Another of my clients, Danielle, watched her start-up fail after a couple of years of hard work. It was heart-wrenching to endure the company's demise, and Danielle definitely had days of total despair; but at some point during the downward spiral, she realized she could glean some very valuable knowledge from the entire experience. She resolved to make the most of her investment—both financial and sweat capital. Currently, Danielle is moving forward on a new project, which fills her with excitement and optimism. Using the work and the experience she gained at her last company and applying it to this new venture, she has turned that failure into a friend.

The next time you experience failure, use this Sweet Spot Check to keep your chin up and learn from the experience.

 SWEET SPOT CHECK **MAKE FAILURE A FRIEND**

- Accept that it hurts to fail, that you may have feelings of sadness or frustration or fear. Give yourself the time and the space to express those feelings. Write them down or share them with people whom you can count on to respond with sympathy and support.

- Resist directing those negative feelings inward or toward others. Avoid playing the blame game, and protect yourself against old self-defeating beliefs. Remember, failing at something does not make you a failure. Choose to emerge from this experience stronger for it.

- Know that this, too, shall pass. While it may be painful, even excruciating, know that the pain will diminish and there will be another stage in your life when you feel the opposite—when you feel tremendous happiness and pride of achievement.

- Take stock of what lessons you can learn. Instead of thinking of yourself as a failure, step back from the experience and identify where it went wrong. What will you know to do differently in the future? Also identify what actually worked along the way, even if you didn't get the results you wanted. Don't throw the baby out with the bathwater!
- Go to bed, putting your mistakes behind you, and wake up the next morning. Greet the new day feeling wiser, less encumbered, and in higher spirits.

Rewrite Your Story

During an inspiring conversation with my good friend Kayla, we discussed our challenges, aspirations, and desires with respect to both our careers and our personal lives. She realized that she'd been telling herself a story that had been holding her back from being totally present and feeling true joy and fulfillment in her personal life. This, not surprisingly, caused strife in her relationship: Kayla was convinced that it was impossible to have both a successful relationship *and* a successful career. She thought she had to choose.

Fortunately, Kayla came to recognize that this was just a fiction she'd been telling herself, not a fact. She now brings the same level of commitment and focus to her relationship as she does to her work. She's chosen both.

I have told myself many stories and believed them wholeheartedly for many years. My biggest and most debilitating story was that I wasn't enough—not good enough, not smart enough, not thin enough, not pretty enough. Another story I told myself was that in a happy relationship, there's no fighting. Previous to that, I believed that fighting a lot indicated a lot of passion. Oy!

What are the stories that you buy into? We tell ourselves hundreds of unproductive stories without even realizing it. To give you a better sense of what I'm talking about, here's a small sampling of stories from my clients:

- "I'm a procrastinator. I can't get things done unless someone pressures me to do so."
- "Once I get rich [skinny/a boyfriend/a promotion], *then* I will be happy."
- "I've always been fat, and I always will be."
- "I am a terrible decision maker. I can't do anything without my wife."
- "I'm totally worthless and will never amount to anything."

- "I was programmed to behave this way."
- "I'm gaining weight because that's just what happens when you age."
- "To be a good mother, I must stay home and tend to my family."
- "I'll never change."
- "He'll never change."
- "Change is impossible at this age."
- "I can't go back to work because I've been out of the industry for too long. I don't know anything anymore."
- "There just isn't a job out there that I can do that I will love."
- "I could never leave this job—I don't know how to do anything else."
- "I could never start a business—I don't know the first thing about it."
- "I never finish anything I start. I don't have what it takes to be successful."
- "All marriages lose their excitement."

Unproductive stories like these could fill volumes. They are fiction—and not the bestseller kind. What story holds you back? Once you figure it out, test it out on your trusted advisors. Determine whether you're being objective, if it stands to reason, or if you can poke holes in it. Then create a new story—one that is much more productive and aligned with your star.

Kayla rewrote her story and has discovered that she *can* have a successful career *and* a happy marriage and home life. A few years later, Kayla and her husband go out on dates regularly, take vacations together, and generally enjoy each other's company in a way that they hadn't in many years. Changing her story has allowed Kayla to be more present and loving with her husband. He appreciates and feels her renewed energy, and together they are much happier.

The story you tell yourself determines whether you get the ending that you want. What fiction might you be telling yourself? Use this Sweet Spot Check to revise your story and create a much more satisfying ending.

SWEET SPOT CHECK **REWRITE YOUR STORY**

- Identify a story that you tell yourself that has determined the way your plot has unfolded to date.
- Share this story with a trusted advisor to hear how it sounds out loud and to see if it stands to reason. Is there any kernel of truth in this story that you can approach from a new perspective, or is it complete fiction? What can you edit out? What new ideas can you incorporate?
- What have you been holding yourself back from because of this story? How has this story blocked you from seeing and achieving what you really want?
- What's the ending you desire, and what is the necessary plot twist that you must implement to get there?

How can you make your story sexier and more exciting, so that you keep coming back for more?

Stop Waiting for Perfect

There is seldom a perfect time to do what you really want to do. And there's no perfect next move. As you now know, I think perfect is for idiots. You can wait forever for all the stars to align, but chances are, they won't. So the question is, what do you do about that? You take the leap.

I recently spoke to a client, Marcie, who was trapped by the need to pursue the perfect thing at the perfect time. She is a typical New York go-getter, beautiful and accomplished. But Marcie was so laser-focused on choosing *exactly* the right opportunity that she couldn't bring herself to make her next move. She was paralyzed. As she sat there in her apartment—surfing the web, doing research, evaluating and analyzing what her strategy would be, perfecting her next step—she was letting life pass her by.

Marcie finally realized that she needed to stop waiting for perfect and take the leap. She needed to stop trying to formulate the foolproof equation for the perfect outcome. Who knew what that would look like, anyway? What good was it doing? She was getting nowhere.

Remember the eight-day seminar I told you about—the one where I completely disconnected from the outside world? I had wanted to attend this seminar for a long time, on the strength of rave reviews from previous participants I knew. I *really* wanted to do this thing. Despite my strong desire, however, there were a couple of issues that stopped me from signing up and actually made me put it off for years.

First, it seemed like a lot of money (in retrospect, in light of the enormous benefits I took away, it now seems like a bargain). It felt like such an indulgence to go off and commune with a bunch of strangers in California for eight days, leaving my family and work responsibilities behind. Yes, I would become a better person, and therefore I would become a better mom, a better wife, and a better coach. But still, I felt a bit selfish wanting to go.

Second, and more pressing, there never seemed to be the perfect time. There were school plays, personal travel, visits from friends and family, birthday parties, holidays, and a full work schedule. That's just the short list. When I finally got the nerve to sign up, I simply took the earliest possible time that my schedule could accommodate, given those limitations. Excellent. Then December rolled around all too quickly, and, as it turned out, it *still* wasn't the perfect time. There were loose ends to tie up, holiday cards to order, end-of-semester special events for the kids, family pictures to take, and a winter vacation to prepare for—let alone all the clients who needed my services. Who was I kidding? December is an incredibly busy time of year!

But still, I went. I reaped tremendous benefits and I rewrote my story. Fittingly, this was where I coined my "Perfect is for idiots" mantra. Here, I learned to embrace chaos and relinquish the quest for perfection that had governed my life. It had been far from perfect timing, but I was forever changed by that week in California. My husband, my kids, my clients, my family, and my friends are all beneficiaries of the kinder, gentler, and more loving person that I am now. I am the biggest beneficiary of all. Had I waited for the perfect time, I would never have gone.

What are *you* putting off because you're waiting for perfect? Don't wait. Take the leap. Do this Sweet Spot Check now.

 SWEET SPOT CHECK   **STOP WAITING FOR PERFECT**

- Identify something you want to do but that you have been holding yourself back from because it's not yet the perfect time.
- Consider whether you are willing to risk *never* doing it by continuing to wait.

- Contemplate all that won't happen, all that you'll surely miss out on, if you continue to wait.
- Consider whether there are additional reasons why you've been waiting (e.g., unproductive stories and beliefs), and see if you can poke holes in them.
- Take the leap! Pick one thing you can do *today* to bring you closer to your objective, then let everything else snowball from there.

Keep Your Paddle Moving

Keep in mind Ellen DeGeneres's voice of adorable Dory in *Finding Nemo*: "Just keep swimming . . . Just keep swimming . . ." Even when you think you've reached your limit, see if you can persevere and push past it. That's where you'll find true magnificence.

While paddleboarding solo in the beautiful waters of Kona, I came to a point where I thought I should head back in. It had been a reasonably long stretch, and I was way out in the water with no one nearby. This was an issue for me on a number of levels. I am an extrovert and love being with people. As much as I appreciate the meditative sound of the water lapping against my paddle and board, paddling alone for as long as I had been pushed my limits. Also, on my paddleboard way out there in the ocean, I had some reasonable fear of encountering animal life, the kind that would be happier to see me than I to see them. To top it off, I was hungry and tired, and thoughts of losing my cushy lounge chair to another aggressive lounge-seeker at the pool came unbidden.

But at the last minute, I decided to keep going. After all, it was only once a year that I was blessed to be in Kona, so I chose to savor all that was exquisite about my favorite Hawaiian island. I went way past the buoys and well beyond my comfort zone. I stopped listening to those voices in my head (*too far . . . too much sun . . . starving . . . arms hurt . . . super thirsty . . . need to pee*) and paddled against the surging current and winds.

As a local girl, I spent years taking the beauty of Hawaii for granted. Lush green mountains? Multiple waterfalls? Rainbows? *Yeah, yeah. Seen 'em all my life.* Turquoise water? Animal life? Abundant sunshine? *Uh-huh. Where's the shade?* I was totally jaded.

But even *I* was totally unprepared for what happened next. As I paddled out farther than I'd ever been, I crossed over into the most spectacular blue I have ever seen—in nature or anywhere else. I couldn't believe how gorgeous this ocean was. In all my years of living in Honolulu and visiting other hard-to-get-to resorts, I had never seen ocean like this. Ever. I was blown away. That jaded local girl? Gone.

When I paddled past the usual Pacific Ocean blue and reached *this* extraordinary blue, which exceeded anything I could've imagined, I actually started laughing and exclaimed out loud to myself, *"Holy shit! This is unbelievable!"* I was *ecstatic!* I'd pushed through my limits—tossing hunger, fatigue, and all reasonableness to the wind—and found myself in this stunning water. *Actually in it*—dipping my paddle into it with every stroke and feeling it splash against my feet.

This is the kind of grace we can all experience when we put in the effort and persevere beyond our limits. This is the kind of magnificence that rewards courage—that awaits us on the far side of our fears and anxieties. This is the laughter and beauty of living in our sweet spot!

Use this Sweet Spot Check to keep your paddle moving. See if you, too, can push through the discomfort and weariness to reach that extraordinary blue.

 SWEET SPOT CHECK   **KEEP YOUR PADDLE MOVING**

- **Notice your desire to stop—what's behind it? Fatigue? Anxiety? Inertia? Do your feelings indicate real cause for concern or are they simply limiting beliefs that have held you back before?**

- **What might you miss out on if you stop now? Can you imagine? Choose to find out by adventuring down this new path.**

- **See if you can push through your limits for just one more stretch. See where that gets you and whether it motivates you to reach for that next stretch (chunk it up!).**

- **Keep your paddle moving—and in that moment when you're on the verge of surrendering, fantasize about what** it will feel like to have reached your destination. Taste the sweetness of achievement and discovery. Invoke your mantra. Do whatever it takes to keep you going.

- Enlist support, if necessary. If you're about to give up, pick up the phone and see if a friend (or a family member, or your coach) can bolster your willpower and help put the wind back in your sail.
- Enjoy your well-deserved moment of grace!

Don't stop just because this is where you've stopped before or because you feel a little discomfort. Silence the negative voices. Keep going even when you think you've had enough. You just never know what astonishing surprise lies on the other side of your extra effort. As my favorite spinning instructor, Rique Uresti, said in one of his classes, "You are always happier than you think you are. More importantly, you are so much stronger than you think you are!" Me? I think you have way more fuel to reach your potential than you think you do. Just keep that paddle moving.

Invoke the Power of Yet

As you're about to close this book, your sweet spot may remain elusive and blurry. You may be keenly aware of what work needs to be done to effect change and to find your sweet spot, but you know you've still got a long journey ahead. Don't be discouraged. Here's where the power of one three-letter word can help you.

Yet.

Add "yet" to the end of any negative statement about what you aren't, what you don't have, what you don't know, or what you can't do, and you'll immediately feel better:

- "I'm so not fit . . . yet."
- "I don't have the job I want . . . yet."
- "I don't have a meaningful relationship . . . yet."
- "I don't know what I need to do . . . yet."
- "I can't control my cravings . . . yet."

Yet. Such a tiny word that wields so much power. It takes an unproductive assertion and converts it to a statement of potential and possibility.

One day, Sloane wanted to play chess, so I suggested she play with her brother. "I don't want to play with Finny," she said. "He's bad at chess!" Indeed, Finn doesn't know how to play chess . . . yet. But as I pointed out to Sloane, that doesn't mean he's bad at chess. For all we know, he could become quite agile on the chessboard. We just need to teach him and then see. He certainly has potential.

Yet. I have seen "yet" blossom into incredible personal transformation for all kinds of people. Even the most skeptical, down-on-their-luck individuals have pursued the power of "yet" to find their sweet spots. I've now shared with you a number of their stories. You're not any different from them or from me. You have yet to see what is possible. This next Sweet Spot Check is super easy and fun. And it will get you into a mindset of possibility.

SWEET SPOT CHECK   INVOKE THE POWER OF YET

Make a list of all the negative things you say to yourself that begin with:

- "I'm not . . ."
- "I don't have . . ."
- "I don't know . . ."
- "I can't . . ."

Review this list and take note of how discouraging and self-limiting you can be. These are the kinds of statements that stop you dead in your tracks.

Add "yet" to the end of each of those sentences. Read them aloud to yourself. Think of each "yet" as a bud of possibility. Imagine, with the right encouragement, how beautifully you will blossom!

This one tiny word can yield a big shift in perspective. Where there was limitation, there is now potential. You have many "yets" in your life. Find out what they are!

Conclusion

Congratulations! You've journeyed a long way toward your sweet spot just by reading this book and executing a number of the Sweet Spot Checks. Now, with all that you have discovered about yourself, and with all of my best tools, tips, and strategies at your fingertips, you have the ability to go the distance—to push beyond all the old beliefs and limitations—to the sweetness and excellence that await.

But do you remember where we started? We started with the imperative that you love yourself—that you cultivate a strong foundation of self-love to support whatever else you build in your life. Remember, I said that if there is one single thing I'd like you to take away from this book, it's that you nurture big love for yourself, just as you do for the people who are most important to you. If you do this one thing, if you keep that love strong and close every single day, all the rest—confidence, gratitude, fulfillment, happiness, and excellence—will come so much more easily.

No matter what your situation, I am optimistic that there is a lot of goodness there to work with, and that now, with some shifts in perspective, you'll be able to see it. Beyond this, it is my great hope that you now have a Technicolor vision of what you want your life to look like—by having mapped out your star and seen it done. Let that vision be your guide. See it. Feel it. Taste it. Always keep it within reach so you'll find the strength, courage, and inspiration to do what you *want* to do, not just what you *should* do.

The Sweet Spot Checks are here for you any time you need them. Use them. Life is a dynamic process. Whether you're aware of it or not, you are always changing; circumstances are constantly shifting. Choose whichever tools come in handy for your next adventure. That's what keeps life interesting! It's the unexpected challenges that call on our agility and excellence. There could be no evolution—personal, professional, or otherwise—without them.

I recognize that it's work. Finding your sweet spot takes commitment. Sometimes it's hard to get motivated. I have watched some of my clients struggle. At times, it's hard for me, too. That's why it's important to have a community of support. Don't go it alone. Find inspiration from your star village—your friends, your family, your colleagues—from me. Avail yourself of the sweet spot resources and community at www.findyoursweetspot.com. Look around at the amazing people and stories that are all around you. Take courage and inspiration from them. Know that through their own struggles, they learned and ultimately reached their desired destinations. Put everything you've got at your disposal into this journey to *your* sweet spot. After all, it is your life we're talking about here. What are you waiting for?

Wishing you sweetness that's spot-on in everything you do!

Acknowledgments

I am thrilled to have had the opportunity to write this book. Thank you to my clients who have given me food for thought, reason, and inspiration to hone and utilize my coaching strategies. I am grateful to you for letting me flex my sweet spot muscles to do what I love to do.

An enormous thank you to my beautiful and amazing friends who gave me the swift kick to begin writing. Christy Evans, Aideen Shortt, and Regina Szpiczynska, I will forever remember going hungry at dinner because you made me take notes on how, specifically, this book would happen.

Major gratitude to Tess Ghilaga, my first editor and dedicated friend, who took on the daunting task of helping me make sense of the words and ideas I put on paper and who affirmed their value as she implemented them in her own life. Great love for Debbie Stevens, who gave me first feedback on the book when I was finally ready to let someone else see it. I love that some of these strategies have become a regular part of our lexicon.

Thank you to Natalia Rose, whose excitement and introduction to Skirt! were critical in this book becoming a reality. To my editor, Anna Bliss, thank you for believing in and pursuing my sweet spot project. Your incisive feedback helped me to shape the text beautifully and with clarity. To other early readers and supporters—Stacey Griffith, Harvey Spevak (and Equinox), Raz Ingrasci, Jay Ferraro, Farel Hruska, Loren Slocum, Sandra Mann, Ellen Ptashek, and Michael Michele—your positive responses to early iterations of this book enhanced my courage to keep working and let others see what I had to say. Thank you!

In addition to Anna, I'm grateful to the Skirt! team, including Sharon Kunz and Ellen Urban, who have worked hard to get this book in tip-top shape and out to the public. To the sweet spot team at DKC, Brooke Hudis, Stephanie Tuck, and Lana Powers, thank you for taking me on and running with all of it from day one. Johnny

Rodriguez and Ria Udaze, together, you make me look good—thank you. Collin Kelly, I'm not sure how I would survive without your technology know-how. And Aideen Shortt and Trisha Lum Attles, thank you for leaning on me to boost my social media effort.

I so appreciate the teachers in my life, particularly at the Hoffman Institute, New York University, and Anthony Robbins. Whether you taught me directly or indirectly, your collective wisdom and insights made it possible for me to have a second and much more satisfying career and contributed to making this book a possibility. A big shout-out to Sharon Kennedy for fortifying my courage in bringing this book to life when execution was just a scintilla of a thought in my brain.

I so appreciate my friends, old and new, far and wide. Our probing conversations about life, beginning in adolescence and continuing into early adulthood and ultimately to this day, lit this spark that has guided my journey. I am so fortunate to have a diverse group of friends who provide such love and kindness, know just what to say to encourage and support me, and make me howl with laughter. Special thanks to Veronica "Queen V" Stigeler and Bill Cowher for your consistently warm support.

Finally, to my family. Thank you to my parents and my brothers for the unyielding love, the gargantuan sacrifices, and the meaningful and fun experiences, all of which have shaped the person I am today. You instilled in me the critical values and the motivation that allow me to achieve, and to be happy.

To Jay, Sloane, and Finn: I have endless love and the deepest gratitude in my heart for each of you and for us as a unit every single day. Jay, your undying belief in and constant support of this book (and, for that matter, all of my endeavors) is sometimes overwhelming. Thank you for encouraging me to pursue my dreams and live in my sweet spot. I really am so lucky. Sloane, thank you for being the catalyst for me wanting to be my best self, for motivating me to look inward and make important change. Finny, thank you for your unconditional love and inspiration. I can only hope to be as kind, expressive, and loving as you are. I am so happy and proud to be a member of our Team Love.

Bibliography

Brooks, Robert B. and Sam Goldstein. *The Power of Resilience: Achieving Balance, Confidence, and Personal Strength in Your Life.* New York: The McGraw Hill Companies, 2004.

Comstock, Kani and Marissa Thame. *Journey to Love: Ten Steps to Wholeness.* Ashland, Oregon: Willow Press, 2000.

Cook, Michelle Schoffro. *The Ultimate pH Solution: Balance Your Body Chemistry to Prevent Disease and Lose Weight.* New York: Collins, an imprint of HarperCollins Publishers, 2008.

Csikszentmihalyi, Mihaly. *Flow: The Psychology of Optimal Experience.* New York: Harper Perennial, Harper Collins, 1990.

Davis, William. *Wheat Belly: Lose the Wheat, Lose the Weight, and Find Your Path Back to Health.* New York: Rodale Books, 2011.

Dweck, Carol S. *Mindset: The New Psychology of Success.* New York: Ballantine Books, an imprint of Random House, Inc., 2006.

Goldsmith, Marshall and Mark Reiter. *What Got You Here Won't Get You There: How Successful People Become Even More Successful.* New York: Hyperion, 2007.

Goleman, Daniel. *Emotional Intelligence: Why It Can Matter More than IQ.* New York: Bantam Dell, a division of Random House, Inc., 2006.

Hay, Louise. *You Can Heal Your Life.* Carlsbad, California: Hay House, Inc., 1999.

Laurence, Tim and Joan Borysenko. *The Hoffman Process: The World Famous Technique That Empowers You to Forgive Your Past, Heal Your Present and Transform Your Future.* New York: Bantam, 2004.

Medina, John. *Brain Rules: 12 Principles for Surviving and Thriving at Work, Home, and School.* Seattle: Pear Press, 2008.

Mehrabian, A., and S. R. Ferris, "Inference of Attitudes from Nonverbal Communication in Two Channels," *Journal of Consulting Psychology,* 31, 3, 48–258 (1967).

Pease, Allan and Barbara. *The Definitive Book of Body Language.* New York: Bantam Dell, a division of Random House, Inc., 2004.

Pink, Daniel H. *Drive: The Surprising Truth about What Motivates Us.* New York: The Penguin Group, 2009.

Pollan, Michael. *In Defense of Food: An Eater's Manifesto.* New York: The Penguin Group, 2008.

Pollan, Michael. *Food Rules: An Eater's Manual.* New York: Penguin Books, 2009.

Ratey, John J. *A User's Guide to the Brain: Perception, Attention, and the Four Theaters of the Brain.* New York: Vintage Books, a division of Random House, Inc., 2001.

Ratey, John J. with Eric Hagerman. *Spark: The Revolutionary New Science of Exercise and the Brain.* New York: Little, Brown and Company, 2008.

Robbins, Anthony. *Unlimited Power: The New Science of Personal Achievement.* New York: Free Press, 1997.

Rock, David. *Quiet Leadership: Six Steps to Transforming Performance at Work.* New York: Harper Collins, 2006.

Rose, Natalia. *Detox 4 Women: An All-New Approach for a Sleek Body and Radiant Health in 4 Weeks.* New York: William Morrow, 2009.

Ruiz, Don Miguel. *The Four Agreements: A Practical Guide to Personal Freedom* (a Toltec Wisdom Book). San Rafael, California: Amber-Allen Publishing, 1997.

Seligman, Martin E. P. *Authentic Happiness: Using the New Positive Psychology to Realize Your Potential for Lasting Fulfillment.* New York: Free Press, a Division of Simon & Schuster, Inc., 2002.

Seligman, Martin E. P. *Flourish: A Visionary New Understanding of Happiness and Well-being.* New York: Free Press, a Division of Simon & Schuster, Inc., 2011.

Sharma, Robin S. *The Monk Who Sold His Ferrari: A Fable about Fulfilling Your Dreams and Reaching Your Destiny.* New York: HarperSanFrancisco, a division of HarperCollins Publishers, 1996.

Shermer, Michael. *The Believing Brain: From Ghosts and Gods to Politics and Conspiracies—How We Construct Beliefs and Reinforce Them as Truths.* New York: Times Books, Henry Holt and Company, 2011.

Slocum, Loren. *Life Tuneups: Your Personal Plan to Find Balance, Discover Your Passion and Step into Greatness.* Guilford, Connecticut: GPP Life, 2009.

Taubes, Gary. *Why We Get Fat: And What to Do about It.* New York: First Anchor Books Edition, a division of Random House, Inc., 2011.

Walker, Norman W. *Become Younger.* Prescott, Arizona: Norwalk Press, 1995.

Whitmore, John. *Coaching for Performance: GROWing People, Performance and Purpose.* London: Nicholas Brealey Publishing, 2007.

Young, Robert O. and Shelley Redford Young. *The pH Miracle: Balance Your Diet, Reclaim Your Health.* New York: Wellness Central, an imprint of Grand Central Publishing, Hachette Book Group USA, Inc., 2002.

Index

About the Author

Karen Elizaga started her career as a corporate lawyer in New York City and then became a corporate executive in London, but she didn't quite land in her sweet spot in either case. After much soul searching, she found her sweet spot as an executive coach and life coach, inspiring, motivating, and empowering individuals for optimal success and happiness. She is the founder of Forward Options.

A natural people person, Karen loves working with a broad range of clients—from stay-at-home mothers and recent high school and college graduates to high-profile executives, lawyers, entrepreneurs, and elite special military operations officers. Across the board, Karen helps her clients find their sweet spots and then define and pursue their next steps toward their dreams with confidence and precision.

In addition to coaching and raising a family, to maintain her sweet spot Karen follows her own advice, carving out time for exercise, fun, and personal exploration, and also serves on the board of the New York Asian Women's Center. Currently, she lives in Manhattan and Westport, Connecticut, with her husband and two children.